GARLAND STUDIES ON

AFRICAN AMERICAN HISTORY AND CULTURE

edited by

GRAHAM HODGES

A GARLAND SERIES

NATIVE SONS IN NO MAN'S LAND

REWRITING AFRO-AMERICAN MANHOOD IN THE NOVELS OF BALDWIN, WALKER, WIDEMAN, AND GAINES

PHILIP AUGER

GARLAND PUBLISHING, Inc.
A MEMBER OF THE TAYLOR & FRANCIS GROUP
NEW YORK & LONDON / 2000

Published in 2000 by
Garland Publishing, Inc.
A Member of the Taylor & Francis Group
29 West 35th Street
New York, NY 10001

10   9   8   7   6   5   4   3   2   1

**Library of Congress Cataloging-in-Publication Data is available
from the Library of Congress.**

Auger, Phillip
Native sons in no man's land : rewriting Afro-American manhood in
the novels of Baldwin, Walker, Wideman, and Gaines / Phillip Auger
    p. cm. – (Garland studies on African American history and culture)
Includes bibliographical references and index.
ISBN: 0-8153-3060-X (alk. paper)

Printed on acid-free, 250-year-life paper
Manufactured in the United States of America

To Kristin
whose love makes all things possible

Contents

Acknowledgments

My eternal gratitude goes out to all who have supported me in the writing of this book. In this brief space I wish to acknowledge those who deserve special thanks: to all of my teachers and advisors who have nurtured my growth as a scholar at U.R.I.; to Sally Burke, Donald Cunnigan, John Leo and Albert Lott for their enthusiasm, support, and advice in making the dissertation happen; to Josie Campbell, my mentor, advisor, and friend, who has taught me as much about integrity as she has about literature. Her support and belief in me throughout my five years of graduate school has taken my scholarship to places I've never thought it could go. To Craig Kleinman, Peter Bayers, and Paul Richards for their lasting friendship and shared enthusiasm about literature; to my family who have never stopped supporting me and have never questioned my ability to reach my goals; and to my wife, Kristin, for putting up with the rollercoaster ride my graduate years have been. More than anything else, her love and faith in me have brought me to this point. I cannot thank her enough.

NATIVE SONS IN NO MAN'S LAND

Looking for Discursive Space in Richard Wright's "No Man's Land"

*What made Bigger's social consciousness most
complex was the fact that he was hovering un-
wanted between two worlds—between powerful
America and his own stunted place in life—and
I took upon myself the task of trying to make the
reader feel this No Man's Land.*
—RICHARD WRIGHT, "HOW 'BIGGER' WAS BORN"

*I was pushing out to new areas of feeling,
strange landmarks of emotion, trampling upon
foreign soil, compounding new relationships of
perceptions, making new and . . . unheard-of
and unfelt effects with words. . . . That is writing
as I feel it, a kind of significant living.*
—RICHARD WRIGHT, "HOW 'BIGGER' WAS BORN"

In the preface to his Amisted collection of critical perspectives on
Richard Wright, Henry Louis Gates, Jr., asserts that "If one had to iden-
tify the single most influential shaping force in modern Black literary
history, one would probably have to point to Wright and the publication
of *Native Son* [1940], his first and most successful novel" (xi). While
Wright's *Native Son* certainly speaks to "the Black experience in America," it more specifically addresses, through the vivid portrayal of its protagonist, Bigger Thomas, the concerns of black men, concerns which
play an important role in all of Wright's fiction. In Bigger Thomas,
Wright's "most influential shaping force" embodies a modern codification of black manhood inscribed as powerless, animalistic, and inarticulate. The dominant racist culture of 1930s Chicago, as it is portrayed in
the novel, discursively segregates Bigger into what Wright himself calls
a *No Man's Land.*

The four writers chosen for this study, James Baldwin, Alice Walker,
John Edgar Wideman, and Ernest Gaines, were chosen because of their

1

shared approach to "rewriting" such negative narratives of black manhood. Each of these writers approaches self-definition and, more specifically, the writing of oneself as a "man" as contingent on controlling discourse—having some power over language—and thus having the power to define the self. And each of the selected works explores the possibilities of black manhoods that are humane and dignified. The discursive negotiations involved in rewriting identity pose an extremely complex set of challenges associated with the realm of definition used to control the powerful signifier, "manhood."

As a "master-narrative" of Afro-American cultural identity, the idea of achieving, or not achieving, one's *manhood* through acts of discursive negotiation is not something that originates with Richard Wright or any of the other writers mentioned above. Gates cites the importance of writing—that is, the control of the language of dominant (white) culture—as key to much of the European debate over slavery in the eighteenth century and to black males being considered "men" ("Writing" 8). Houston A. Baker, Jr., in *The Journey Back*, gives some perspective to the task of the slave attempting to "write himself into existence":

> the slave narrator must . . . accomplish the almost unthinkable . . . task
> of transmuting an authentic, unwritten self—a self that exists outside
> the conventional literary discourse structures of the white reading pub-
> lic—into literary representation. . . . Once he has seized the public
> medium, the slave narrator can construct a public message . . . calcu-
> lated to win approval for himself. (168)

Bigger Thomas's "lack of manhood," in this context, is due to his inability to participate in "conventional discourse structures"; he is unable to seize the public medium which objectifies him. As Baker suggests, "seizing" the public medium is an "unthinkable" task, and, often, "discursive negotiations," rhetorical acts working through and around dominant language, prove to be the way to manhood. Richard Yarborough stresses the significance of "manhood" as a cultural signifier which, as much if not more so than any other signifier, is "essentially ideologically charged . . . serving, first to bolster the self-image of privileged whites who endorsed and propagated it through their control of major acculturating institutions and, second, to keep marginalized those 'others' who—on account of their appearance, speech, family background, class, religion, behavior, or values—did not measure up" (168). This being the case, Yarborough finds in his study of Frederick Douglass and other Afro-American male writers of the nineteenth century that becoming understood as "manly" within the dominant discourses of America isn't simply biologically determined for black men. Instead, manly identity required social negotiations through a discursive battlefield—what John Edgar Wideman calls the "battle to define reality."

Perhaps the most influential Afro-American slave narrative, that of Frederick Douglass, has significance here. Douglass cites his becoming literate and ultimately "writing his own life," as a validation of his manhood. His ability to tell readers himself "how the slave was made man" is proof in itself that he *is*. James Olney writes that "the ability to utter his name, and more significantly the ability to utter it in the mysterious characters on the page . . . is what Douglass' *Narrative* is all about, for in that lettered utterance is assertion of identity and in identity is freedom"(54).

In the twentieth century, W.E.B. Dubois's call to black men, "if they are really men," to oppose white "civilizing methods" and to see "advancement" through the promotion of higher education takes on resonance as well (*Souls* 40). The message of Dubois is the same as that of Douglass: the achievement of "manhood" comes from the act of entering into and at least partially controlling discourse and modes of representation, having power over language with which to represent and define oneself. Richard Wright refers to such control of language as the point at which life becomes meaningful—significant living.

It is worth noting that with dominant white culture inscribed by the discourse of patriarchy, the key to empowerment in much of Afro-American literature is the appropriation of the "discourse of manhood," in the gendered sense, not simply of "humanity." Calvin Hernton, in *The Sexual Mountain and Black Women Writers* points to what may be considered the irony of a gendered position (i.e. manhood) being a major signifying force within a struggle that is primarily racial:

> Historically the battle line of racial struggle in the United States has been drawn exclusively as a struggle between the men of the races. Everything having to do with the race has been defined and counter-defined by the men as a question of whether black people were or were not a race of Men. The central concept and the universal metaphor around which all aspects of the racial situation revolve is [sic] "Manhood." (38)

While such a system of empowerment is obviously central to the marginalization and disempowerment of women, both black and white, the racism informing the discourse of manhood is also a significant problem for black men.

It is important to make clear the notion of discourse which permeates this study and to clarify its significance in Wright's *Native Son*. *Discourse* as I use it is borrowed from Michel Foucault's *The Archaeology of Knowledge*. He defines discourse as expressions of language which, depending on the subject position of its agent, can be a tool of great social power. He sees the control of discourse as ultimately the power within language to present and sanction truth. That power is socially determined through a network of cultural authorization involving all of what Yarborough calls the "major acculturating institutions" of society including familial, legislative, medical, judiciary, educational, and even religious establishments:

> . . . discourse is not the majestically unfolding manifestation of a thinking, knowing, speaking subject, but, on the contrary, a totality. . . . (50)

With this in mind, the task of a black male becoming understood as a man, by dominant society or even by himself, requires effecting—a "totality" of discursive relations surrounding him. In Wright's *Native Son*, Bigger Thomas is confined, figuratively and literally, in a discursive totality which doesn't recognize his legitimacy or his manhood. More to the point, he has no access to the hegemonic discourses that dominate his world. The black culture Wright addresses is one that is effectively disenfranchised by the dominant discourse of white racism of the early twentieth century, what Wright calls "a whole panoply of rules, taboos, and penalties" designed to "keep Blacks in their place" ("Bigger" xii). The dominant discourses of the Jim Crow culture in the South and urban racial depression in the North were informed by a "vast, dense ideology of racial superiority that would justify any act of violence against [blacks] to defend white dominance" (xii).

In the face of the oppression of racist dominant discourse is Bigger. He is described by Wright in "How 'Bigger' was Born" as a "dispossessed and disinherited man," one who is "not yet articulate," "longing for self-identification" (xx). Wright makes clear that Bigger's inarticulateness, his inability to control discourse, keeps him from legitimacy and manhood. Wright notes that Bigger Thomas was a "distinct type" of black man who revolted against white society for two reasons:

> First, through some quirk of circumstances, he had become estranged from the religion and the folk culture of his race. Second, he was trying

to react to and answer the call of the dominant civilization whose glitter came to him through the newspapers, magazines, radios, movies, and the mere imposing sight and sound of daily American life. (xiii)

Bigger as a "distinct type" of black manhood is estranged from those discourses which could provide him with a more "human" sense of identity. Just as Bigger and the black community of Chicago in the 1930s are segregated into impoverished living spaces, or ghettos, discourse also acts to segregate them from power. Racist discourses he must "react" to are contained in the "glitter," or ideology, of white racism and controlled by white modes of representation, the "discursive spaces" in which ideology is largely produced and transmitted. Instead of having some control over language and comfortably using the dominant discourse to attain a more positive sense of self-definition, Bigger, according to Wright, is placed outside of a "culture which could hold or claim his allegiance and faith." Wright refers to him as "stranded, a free agent to roam the streets of our cities, a hot and whirling vortex of undisciplined and unchannelized impulses" (xix). Bigger is "uprooted" by dominant discourse, not empowered by it.

Houston Baker, Jr., in an essay on Wright entitled (aptly) "On Knowing our Place," gives much attention to the correspondence between Bigger's being "bereft of determinative control" and his being "placed":

If one . . . is constituted and maintained by and within boundaries set by the dominant authority, then one is not the setter of place but the prisoner of another's desire. Under the displacing impress of authority even what one calls and, perhaps, feels is one's *own place* is, from the perspective of human agency, *placeless*. Bereft of determinative control of boundaries, the occupant of authorized boundaries would not be secure in his or her own eulogized world but maximally secured by another, a prisoner of interlocking, institutional arrangements of power. (201)

These "interlocking, institutional arrangements of power" are what Wright refers to as "a whole panoply of rules, taboos, and penalties." Ultimately, Bigger is both outside of any discourse that might empower him and entrapped in the discourse of white racism which defines him as something less than a man. He is "placed" effectively in a "No Man's Land."

Richard Wright remarks that it is in the face of an absence of a validating discourse that he became "more than ever resolved toward the task of creating with words a scheme of images and symbols [a discourse] whose direction could enlist the sympathies, loyalties and yearnings of the millions of Bigger Thomases in every land and race . . ." (xix). The creation of *Native Son* for Wright is, in effect, the creation of a discursive space for his own use of language to counter the power of the discourse(s) of dominant culture. Wright refers to the "newspapers, magazines, radios, movies, and the mere imposing sight and sound of daily American life" as the "totality" of discursive space covered by white discourse. But with the creation of the novel, *Native Son*, Wright shows that "breaches" in discursive totalities do exist, that discourses are not as fixed as they appear to be. Wright creates discursive space for his own voice to be heard and for his own legitimacy as a black man and novelist to be recognized. In his act of creation, the creation of the novel itself, Wright reproduces hope, opening more discursive space for future acts of black male self-determination.

Bigger Thomas, however, remains a modern codification of black manhood imprisoned in a literal and discursive cage, unable to "write" (control) his destiny, awaiting his death. When Bigger does react against the oppressive environment around him, with his killing of Mary Dalton and the rape and murder of his girlfriend, Bessie, the result is a warped attempt at "becoming a man," an appropriation of "the discourse of manhood" that defines a man by his misogynistic acts. Houston Baker cites Bigger's rape and murder of Bessie as the "bigger man (of Western culture) in the making." Bigger's perception of his act reveals his feeling that he was "backed into a corner":

> Had he raped [Mary]? Yes he had raped her . . . But rape was not what one did to women. Rape was what one felt when one's back was against the wall and one had to strike out, whether one wanted to or not, to keep the pack from killing one. (qtd. in Baker 221)

Baker asserts that the "signal presence" of rape is the "archi-sign of white-male authority and domination" (221) and that "Bessie's raped and murdered body is witness at the conclusion of *Native Son* to black men's mistaken notions about flight" (223):

> Bigger becomes readable as a parodic, black repetition of the male principle of Western ascendancy that Wright celebrates as the genesis of modernism. (222)

Baker's points in mind, Bigger's destruction and fragmentation of Mary Dalton become readable as the inevitable result of "undisciplined and unchannelized impulses," of being backed into a corner. In this case is Bigger attempting to *hack* breaches into white discourse? to *burn* its influence completely? He is entrapped in the overwhelming "totality" of white racist discourse. He never finds, nor can produce, the "breach" in discourse which will allow him to articulate or "rewrite" his identity. Bigger's "undisciplined and unchannelized impulses" only serve to reinforce problematic "male principles of Western ascendancy" and white racist stereotypes about black males.

Ultimately, *Native Son* is an indictment against a society that, through the subtle and pervasive powers of discursive hegemony, makes no space for Bigger. Wright believes that such hegemony has breaches (spaces or gaps in language) in which one can begin to "rewrite" discourse. *Native Son* itself is testament to the transformability of language with its potential for revolution. But the Bigger Thomases of the world often realistically fail where Wright himself succeeds.

With the studies of selected novels by Baldwin, Walker, Wideman, and Gaines, I wish to uncover what I see as a movement in more contemporary Afro-American fiction toward examining the discursive politics involved in the rewriting, or "reW*right*ing," of such powerless, inarticulate versions of black manhood as that codified by Wright in Bigger Thomas. These four contemporary novelists all recognize a great deal to be at stake in the discursive construction of manhood. I do not propose that all of the works of fiction discussed are rewritings focused specifically at Richard Wright's novel, but there is an unavoidable intertextuality at play in these novels. Clearly, an important element which these novels share is the evidence in each to suggest that Wright's depiction of Bigger Thomas in *Native Son* has been a (if not *the*) major voice informing them. The novels treated in this study present their writers sharing a desire to transcend the discursive boundaries that control mainstream American definitions of (Black) manhood. James Baldwin expresses such a desire for transcendence in reaction to *Native Son*, and his concerns are indicative of all of the novelists of this study. He sees the inability to confront dominant discursive control as central to what he calls the "tragedy" of Bigger Thomas and the "failure" of *Native Son* as a protest novel:

> . . . For Bigger's tragedy is . . . that he has accepted the theology that
> denies him life, that he admits the possibility of his being sub-human

> and feels constrained. . . . The failure of the protest novel lies . . . in its
> insistence that it is his categorization alone which cannot be tran-
> scended. ("Everybody's" 22-3)

Although it remains debatable whether Baldwin's work or any of the
novels of this study (including *Native Son*) actually presents alternative
"theologies" which revolutionize the dominant discourse so that black
men have discursive space as well as white men, each novel at least presents its own statement about the discursive negotiations necessary for
such revolution (transcendence) to occur. It is the modernized black male
victim of white social construction, especially as he is depicted in
Wright's *Native Son*, who provides the impetus for the "post-modern"
rewritings which are the subject of this study.

The notion of "realizing discursive transcendence" presents "postmodern" complications and needs some unpacking as well. *Post-mod-
ernism*, as the term is used in this study, presents what James W.
Coleman, in his book about John Edgar Wideman, *Blackness and Modernism*, calls "fictions," "arbitrary appropriations of language" that do
not present, or attempt to present, reality in any objective or universal
way. Instead, one's sense of "truth" only becomes "real" in the context of
the discursive formation in which it is grounded. Terry Eagleton, in his
theorizing about a postmodern rhetorical foundation of reality and truth,
contextualizes this relationship as follows:

> To say that [a text] is 'true' is not to state that it represents a real state of
> affairs. It is to claim that the text so fictionalizes the 'real' as to intend a
> set of effects conducive to certain practices that are deemed, in light of
> a particular set of falsifiable hypotheses about the nature of society, to
> be desirable. . . . (113)

If all truth is based on relational discursive formations, the way to redefining a "reality" or a self-identity, then, is by shifting the discursive
foundation upon which definition rests.

This method of "rewriting" reality is at the heart of the strategy
toward change I see in place for the four writers of fiction presented in
this study. In an interview conducted by James Coleman in 1988, John
Edgar Wideman presents his own strategy at redefining reality through
his control of discourse in his fiction:

> . . . both plots and themes of the fictions I write, and the fictions them-
> selves, are an attempt to subvert one notion of reality with others, to

show that there is not simply one way of seeing things but many ways of seeing things. And as a people and as individuals if we don't jump into the breach, if we don't fight the battle to define reality in our own terms, then somebody else will come along and do it for us. (152)

I wish to make it clear that in "subverting one notion of reality with others" Baldwin, Walker, Wideman, and Gaines share the realization that the foundation of discursive relations must be subverted first. In the postmodern world of these writers, their concern is not so much to "establish truth," a notion that doesn't recognize the power within language to produce change, as it is to struggle for livable meanings and realities.

Chapter One of this study discusses James Baldwin's *Giovanni's Room* (1956). Although this novel's protagonist is a white man with blond hair whose "ancestors conquered a continent," *Giovanni's Room* is Baldwin's attempt at finding new discursive space for himself as an artist and as a black man. He writes that " . . . to become a Negro man, let alone a Negro artist, one had to make oneself up as one went along. This had to be done in the not-so-metaphorical teeth of the world's determination to destroy you. The world had prepared no place for you, and if the world had its way, no place would exist" (233). *Giovanni's Room*, written during the early period of Baldwin's career as a novelist and along side his *Notes of a Native Son*, can and should be read as part of Baldwin's reaction to the limitations of self-determinism he finds to be the failure of Richard Wright's *Native Son*. In "Everybody's Protest Novel" Baldwin notes that Wright fails as a protest novelist because the "acts of creation" of his protagonist, Bigger Thomas, work only as "a continuation, a complement of the monstrous legend [*Native Son*] was written to destroy" (22). From Baldwin's point of view, Bigger never overcomes the power of dominant discourse that defines him in stereotypically subhuman terms. He remains trapped, literally and discursively, in the space dominant culture has deemed appropriate for him.

The protagonist of *Giovanni's Room*, David, is in a state of ambivalence about his sexual identity; the dominant discourse of American patriarchy that his father represents doesn't include terms which define him, and part of his trip to France is "to find himself." David has "no space," physically, geographically, or discursively, to express his homosexuality freely. He is left in a "web of ambiguity," constantly trying to evade any fixed notion of his sexual identity because that identity is likely to keep him ostracized from mainstream culture.

For Baldwin, however, creating a new discursive space for himself as a novelist, and as a homosexual black man, proves to be a large part of his producing and publishing *Giovanni's Room*. In creating a novel that links black masculinity with homosexuality, Baldwin not only takes on the dangers of publicly "coming out of the closet," but he insists on expanding the possibilities for the way society conceives of Black manhood. In effect he discursively positions himself in his own literal "no man's land." For his character, David, such a position produces nothing but fear and evasion, but for himself as a novelist, Baldwin found no other way of producing change through literature. Responding to the failure to overcome the "reality bequeathed us at our birth" that he finds characterizes Wright's *Native Son*, he writes:

> We take our shape, it is true, within and against that cage of reality bequeathed us at our birth; and yet it is precisely through our dependence on this reality that we are most endlessly betrayed. Society is held together by our need; we bind it together with legend, myth, coercion, fearing that without it we will be hurled into that void, within which, like the earth before the Word was spoken, the foundations of society are hidden. From the void—ourselves—it is the function of society to protect us; but it is only this void, our unknown selves, demanding, forever, a new act of creation, which can save us. ("Everybody's" 20-1)

In order to avoid the "cage of reality" that keeps Bigger Thomas in a state of literal and discursive bondage, one must find a "void," literally a gap or absence of language, in which to create new discursive space and new options for defining reality—for "rewriting," and in this case, specifically for "reW*right*ing," manhood.

Alice Walker's *The Third Life of Grange Copeland* (1970) is a statement similar to Baldwin's about finding discursive space from which to redefine manhood. For Walker as a woman and a feminist, there is a great deal at stake in the discursive "battle" over cultural inscriptions of manhood. *The Third Life of Grange Copeland* is a response to what bell hooks calls "the rather politically naive and dangerous assumption that it is in the interests of black liberation to support sexism and male domination" (101). Grange Copeland and his son Brownfield initially attempt to define themselves as men by violently lashing out at women. In such acts, Grange and Brownfield initially take the same misogynistic path toward "manhood" that Bigger is famous for, but Grange does "rewrite" a sense of manly identity out of what Baldwin refers to as a "void" of language—what Walker refers to as Grange's "dispassionate vacancy."

In buying and fencing off a farm, Grange demarks his own space from which he can produce a new ideology of manhood which will not reproduce monstrous legends. In this space, Grange changes from speaking only with shrugs to becoming an articulate inventor and teller of folk tales. He takes advantage of his farm, a representation of his discursive space, to subvert traditional usages of language and notions of manhood, and he creates a new self out of the breach of dominant white influence.

The result of Grange's rewriting of manhood is not exactly utopic, however, as questions remain about his effect on the "real" world outside the fenced-off space of his farm. Both Grange and Brownfield die before the novel's end, but Grange's granddaughter, Ruth, moves forth into the "real world" looking for more "discursive space" in which to spread Grange's hopeful ideology. Ultimately, Walker's novel is an important questioning about the limits of social and discursive change and the extent to which "rewritings" of black manhood take up more than "merely" aesthetic space.

John Edgar Wideman's 1990 novel *Philadelphia Fire* is the subject of *Chapter Three*. Many of Wideman's writings from the late sixties to the present are autobiographically driven, about urban black men, like Bigger Thomas, trying to negotiate an empowered sense of manhood. In *Philadelphia Fire*, Wideman explores the frustration involved for black men attempting to rewrite debilitating narratives of black manhood that have led to their alienation and silence.

Philadelphia Fire is centered around an actual event, the 1985 fire-bombing of an Afro-American radical communal group resulting in the deaths of eleven people, five of whom were children. In the actual event, and in Wideman's depiction of it, a child escapes from the massacre, and it is the boy who escapes—whom Wideman calls Simba—that becomes the obsession of the novel's protagonist, Cudjoe. Cudjoe is a blocked writer who, similar to Baldwin's David, sees no life for himself in America and tries to "find himself" in Europe. After ten years of little progress it is the fire in Philadelphia that brings him back to his home town with the intention of writing about the boy who has escaped. Cudjoe knows that Simba has the potential of taking on great symbolic and mythological status, perhaps becoming the focal point of a new revolutionary discourse for the Black population in Philadelphia. Yet, Cudjoe remains unable to write, unable to provide the discourse, or to find the discursive space, necessary for change.

Wideman presents a fragmented and disjointed narrative in which Cudjoe is often portrayed as being entrapped by discourse. His unsuccessful attempt to stage a production of Shakespeare's *The Tempest* is what Wideman calls the center of the novel, and it provides further evidence of the frustration involved in rewriting identity. Cudjoe's hope to rewrite and stage Shakespeare's play is similar to his desire to write about the fire, but in this instance, as in others, he fails in his ability to use language: he cannot rise above his own "will-lessness" and instability as a narrator. In fact, Wright's depiction of Bigger as "a hot and whirling vortex of undisciplined and unchannelized impulses" is an especially fitting description of Cudjoe who can't find the stability to write, or rewrite, his identity in the face of the *tempestuous* forces of social disenfranchisement. Cudjoe's response to suggestions by his friends to produce a more radical revision of the play is a telling statement about his and others' inability to use language to produce change:

> You can't just rewrite *The Tempest* any old way you please. . . . Play got to end as it always does. Prospero still the boss. Master of ceremonies. Spinning the wheel of fortune. Having the last laugh. Standing there thinking he's cute telling everybody what to do next. And people can't wait to clap their hands and say thanks. (144)

At the novel's end, Simba is not found, but he does remain "out there," possibly to be the transgressive "fabulator" of new narratives that will bring about discursive change. Still, *Philadelphia Fire* presents the act of rewriting manhood as frustrated by debilitating social conditions and racist discourses about Blacks, and also by a "will-lessness" on the part of Blacks—brought on by such frustration—to make any attempt at discursive agency.

Ultimately Wideman's message is, like Wright's, mixed about the power of Blacks to rewrite manhood. Whereas his protagonist presents a largely pessimistic picture of himself, and of Blacks in general, Wideman remains hopeful about his own potential as a writer to be transgressive. Wideman's radically liberating use of narrative technique is evidence that, contrary to Cudjoe's insistence otherwise, tales can be told in more than one way. And his conception of his fiction being "an attempt to subvert one notion of reality with another" remains an important force in *Philadelphia Fire*.

Ernest Gaines' 1993 novel, *A Lesson Before Dying*, in many ways reenacts the social situation presented in Wright's *Native Son* of an inarticulate black man being victimized and imprisoned by white authority. The novel is narrated by Grant, a black school teacher from a Southern sharecropping community ruled by Jim Crow laws. His goal is to help

Jefferson, a poor uneducated black man, realize a sense of manhood—a difficult task considering Jefferson has been wrongfully accused of murder and sentenced to death. Whereas many of Gaines' novels address the issue of establishing manhood, *A Lesson Before Dying* is distinct in that it focuses on this issue in a most direct way: the problem Grant and Jefferson are faced with is a problem of redefining Jefferson. He is identified, for all intents and purposes, as a hog by his own white lawyer. The members of the black community work together to redefine him as a man.

Throughout the novel Gaines presents many obstacles preventing such redefinition, including a Wideman-like "will-lessness" on the part of Grant who feels powerless (unmanly) himself. He has a better education than most if not all of the population of his community, white and black, yet he feels powerless to effect change as a teacher of blacks in that community. Gaines shows that it is the white patriarchal elite of the community, the group that controls social structures, who also control the discursive structures which are in place to preserve white forms of power. These structures are the manifestations of power to which Foucault refers when he speaks of discursive totality. For black members of this southern community, such structures of white patriarchy are there to disempower, to convict, to imprison, and to enslave.

With such imprisoning discursive structures in place, the objective of Grant, Jefferson, and the rest of the black community is to penetrate the "cage" of white-supremacist discourse—something attempted but never fully realized in *Native Son*. In *A Lesson Before Dying*, however, Grant and the others are successful not only in penetrating a "discursive cage" but also in instilling a new mythology based on the manhood of Jefferson. The resulting discourse takes on religious dimensions as Jefferson is understood by the community as a Christ-figure who provides his own "new testament" to the legitimacy of his manly identity. His power to redeem and redefine, verified by the love and support of his family and community, effectively combats the frustration and "will-lessness" that originally made transformation impossible.

With Jefferson never physically escaping the confines of his imprisonment and dying just as Bigger Thomas does, Gaines' novel, like the others of this study, presents a less than utopic rewriting of black manhood. However, his rewriting is the most hopeful yet about the potential for black men to break through the "prison-house of language" of white racist patriarchy. More so than any of the other works of this study, Gaines responds to Baldwin's call not to accept a "theology that denies him life." His protagonist appropriates Christian theology, "The Word," the foundational structure of discourse, to arrive at "justification through faith" in the "new testament" which proclaims his manhood.

The four novels chosen for this study all "speak to each other" and "signify on" Wright's portrayal of Bigger Thomas in *Native Son.* Their intertextuality creates its own "discursive space" in the wake of influence of Richard Wright's "most influential shaping force." I hope that this dissertation will open doors to make this space even greater. I believe it reveals a great deal about the American and specifically Afro-American obsession with manly identity, about the segregation of voices within discursive space, and about the power of language to shape identity.

CHAPTER 1

James Baldwin: Rewriting from the Closet

Looking for Discursive Space in *Giovanni's Room*

> *It is the power of revelation which is the busi-*
> *ness of the novelist, this journey toward a more*
> *vast reality which must take precedence over all*
> *other claims.*
>
> —JAMES BALDWIN,
> "EVERYBODY'S PROTEST NOVEL"

> *It seems to me that nature does not help us very*
> *much when we need illumination in human*
> *affairs. I am certainly convinced that it is one*
> *of the greatest impulses of mankind to arrive*
> *at something higher than a natural state. How*
> *to be natural does not seem to me to be a prob-*
> *lem—quite the contrary. The great problem is*
> *how to be—in the best sense of that kaleido-*
> *scopic word—a man.*
>
> —JAMES BALDWIN, "THE MALE PRISON"

Much of James Baldwin's writing addresses issues concerning the construction of manhood, but his second novel, *Giovanni's Room*, is perhaps his most substantial statement about manhood in that its protagonist struggles to achieve a sense of masculine identity with which he can be comfortable and be accepted by society. As the title of the work suggests, *Giovanni's Room* is about a space, more specifically, the physical and discursive space, (not) made for its protagonist, David, to express his sexuality freely. The novel is organized in a confessional manner in which David tells of his life's ordeal of trying to negotiate a sense of manhood which is acceptable to both his social and "natural" selves. Although David is not a black man (he has blond hair and his "ancestors conquered a continent"), the anxiety he wrestles with over his sexual identity signifies on Baldwin's own "negotiations of manhood." In the process of this novel, Baldwin foregrounds the issue of finding and escaping "spaces," be it Giovanni's "room," the "space" of David's American home, or the "closeted space" of discursive containment.

An objective of this chapter is to examine Baldwin's presentation of external and internal spaces which act metaphorically to signify the "discursive space" David needs to be author to his own identity. Also, I wish to establish David's struggle as largely symbolic of Baldwin's own struggle to author his own identity as not *"merely* a Negro; or, even, merely a Negro writer."* To a great extent, *Giovanni's Room* reflects Baldwin's negotiations with language to find his own space within language—in effect, to come out of the closet, to establish a new discursive foundation for producing a positive sense of meaning in being an Afro-American novelist and an Afro-American man.

After his initial success with the publication of *Go Tell It On The Mountain,* many felt that the safest way for Baldwin to develop as a successful Afro-American novelist would be continue writing about "Afro-American concerns." *Giovanni's Room,* of course, does not do this. The novel does not include an Afro-American character, and homosexual subject matter placed Baldwin in a literal "no-man's land" into which publishers were hesitant to go. As W.J. Weatherby points out,

> One of [Baldwin's] most traumatic experiences was the fate of *Giovanni's Room. . . .* He had been made to tone down the homosexual ending of the first novel, but there was no way the theme of homosexuality could be cut out of the second novel. . . . It would merely be a homosexual novel to most people, even publishers. In 1955, when the majority of American homosexuals found it much safer to remain in the closet, the reaction to the homosexual novel was predictable. . . .
> (117-18)

Weatherby's biography of Baldwin includes the remarks of one of the editors working for Alfred Knopf: "He was a black writer, which isn't easy, and [*Giovanni's Room*] would have given him the identity of a black homosexual writer. Of course now no one would think twice about such a book. We've moved on" (135). Such remarks make it clear that Afro-American male novelists, as Afro-Americans, as men, and as novelists, were, to a large extent, confined to specific "discursive spaces" by the expectations of publishers and their reading audiences. They also make clear that representations of masculinity played a large role in the cultural license given to Afro-American male writers of the 1950s.

David Savran, writing about the politics of masculinity in 1950s America, writes that the post war ideology of familialism and the theory of "sex roles" "severely disparaged and marginalized" those who did not conform to normative constructions of masculinity and femininity. Citing Elaine Tyler May's *Homeward Bound: American Families in the Cold War Era*, he writes that the 1950s brought on "an intensive level of surveillance posted over the circulation of sexuality in and around the nuclear family [facilitating] an unprecedented level of social control," what May calls the "domestic version of containment" (6-7). Against this backdrop is Baldwin, who is not only trying to find a discursive space for homosexuality to be accepted, but who is also trying to redefine what he sees as Wright's confirmation of racist stereotypes of the animalistic overaggressive black man.

Baldwin's own remarks in "The Black Boy Looks at the White Boy," first published in *Esquire* in 1961, tells a great deal about the extent to which Baldwin's concerns for his freedom of expression as a man were intertwined with his similar concerns as a writer:

> . . . . to become a Negro man, let alone a Negro artist, one had to make oneself up as one went along. This had to be done in the not-so-metaphorical teeth of the world's determination to destroy you. The world had prepared no place for you, and if the world had its way, no place would exist. (233)

Even though *Giovanni's Room* does not include a "Negro man," the problems David faces are best defined the same way: "no place"—except closeted, contained places—exists for him either. Stephen Porter's claim that to Baldwin issues of sexual and racial containment in America are "hopelessly intertwined" (153) most appropriately describes the politics of containment in *Giovanni's Room*.

To lend some perspective to Baldwin's interest in making a new discursive space for black male self-determination, it is important to consider Baldwin's concerns in "Everybody's Protest Novel," originally published in 1949 and reprinted in his collection of essays, *Notes of a Native Son*, in 1955, only a year before the publication of *Giovanni's Room*. Of course, as the collection's name would suggest, *Notes of a Native Son* focuses a great deal of attention on Richard Wright's novel, *Native Son*. In particular, the collection's first two essays, "Everybody's Protest Novel" and "Many Thousands Gone" take issue with Wright's presentation of Bigger Thomas, the central character, in what Baldwin

calls "the most powerful and celebrated statement we have yet had of
what it means to be a Negro in America" ("Thousands" 30). Baldwin
shows great concern in "Everybody's Protest Novel" for Wright's natu-
ralistic presentation of the inescapability of Bigger's confinement within
racist systems of categorization:

> We take our shape, it is true, within and against that cage of reality be-
> queathed us at our birth; and yet it is precisely through our dependence
> on this reality that we are most endlessly betrayed. Society is held to-
> gether by our need; we bind it together with legend, myth, coercion,
> fearing that without it we will be hurled into that void, within which,
> like the earth before the Word was spoken, the foundations of society
> are hidden. From the void—ourselves—it is the function of society to
> protect us; but it is only this void, our unknown selves, demanding, for-
> ever, a new act of creation which can save us—'from the evil that is in
> the world.' (20-1) . . . For Bigger's tragedy is . . . that he has accepted
> the theology that denies him life, that he admits the possibility of his
> being sub-human and feels constrained. . . . The failure of the protest
> novel lies . . . in its insistence that it is his categorization alone which
> is real and which cannot be transcended. (22-3)

At least two issues in the above remarks are significant in relation to
Baldwin's writing of *Giovanni's Room*. First, Baldwin raises the issue of
"the void," an empty space "into" which one would fear to be "hurled."
Baldwin notes that it is through acts of discursive agency, the control of
legend, myth, coercion, that one finds safe spaces; but even those "safe
spaces" are often found in discursive cages of categorization—theologies—put forth by dominant ideological forces working to determine
identity. Second, while Baldwin faults Wright for presenting ideological
categorization as the only reality which cannot be transcended, Baldwin
remains ambiguous about the shape such transcendence would take—
what place does one inhabit if one is in the void?—and it is questionable
whether Baldwin presents any such transcendence for any of the characters in *Giovanni's Room*.

Another significant issue addressed in "Everybody's Protest Novel"
is Baldwin's recognition of the identity of black manhood as a central element in the cage of Bigger's categorization. To escape the overwhelming social determination that defines him in "monstrous" terms, Bigger is
driven to murder and rape, and "through this violence, we are told, for
the first time, to a kind of life, having for the first time redeemed his man-

hood"(22). For Baldwin, Wright's failure as a protest novelist lies in Bigger's "acts of creation" only working as "a continuation, a complement of the monstrous legend it was written to destroy" (22). This sentiment is repeated in "Alas, Poor Richard," published as part of *Nobody Knows My Name* in 1961:

> Thus, when in Wright's pages a Negro male is found hacking a white woman to death, the very gusto with which this is done, and the great attention paid to the details of physical destruction reveal a terrible attempt to break out of the cage in which the American imagination has imprisoned him for so long. (188)

Ultimately, Baldwin asserts, negative dehumanizing myths of black manhood are reaffirmed, with little, if any, suggestion that transcendence is possible. My point here is not to suggest that Baldwin found no redeeming qualities in *Native Son*, nor is it necessarily to affirm Baldwin's reading of the novel; instead, I wish to present Baldwin's concerns for creating new representational forms which will in turn provide the discursive foundations for more positive "acts of creation." Such concerns bear great weight in informing both his writing of *Giovanni's Room* and his presentation of himself as an Afro-American man and novelist.

    Giovanni's Room shares a theme with *Native Son* in that David, like Bigger, tries to transcend ideological categorization—dominant "versions of containment." In David's case, the force with which he is forever struggling is the voice of his father: "all I want for David is that he grow up to be a man. And when I say man, . . . I don't mean a Sunday school teacher"(24). His father's attempts to be precise in defining "man" and his aunt Ellen's objection that "a man is not the same thing as a bull" serve to present manhood as a signifier which is unstable for David. The ambivalence of his father and his aunt in defining their versions of healthy manhood presents them as participating in what Baldwin calls "making oneself up as one [goes along]," and their problems in articulating manhood leave David in a state of ambivalence about his identity. What David does know is that he would feel more freedom with some "merciful distance" from his father's conception of healthy manhood. David narrates that he went to France "perhaps . . . to find myself," a statement he also has trouble defining: "this is an interesting phrase, . . . which certainly does not mean what it says but betrays a nagging suspicion that something has been misplaced"(31). David's geographic move from America to France is an attempt to actively *expatriate* himself from his father's patriarchal strictures. In doing so he attempts to experience at least a more autonomous, if also experimental, identity. Like Baldwin's assertion about the "business of the novelist," David's "business" in moving is to attempt a "journey toward a more vast reality which must take precedence over all other claims."

But what David finally realizes about his "journey" is that he is actually involved in escaping placement: "I had decided to allow no room in the universe for something which shamed or frightened me, I succeeded very well—by not looking at the universe, by not looking at myself, by remaining, in effect, in constant motion" (30-31). What David attempts to create out of the void (that is the self) is an act to save him from the hegemonic discourses of the world that imprison him either as a "bull" or a "Sunday school teacher." He doesn't seem able to do this; he can only remain in flight, in motion. While David feels anxiety about being "misplaced," his attempts "to find himself" are actually centered on the creation of "elaborate systems of evasion":

> People who believe that they are strong willed and the masters of their destiny can only continue to believe this by becoming specialists in self-deception. Their decisions are not really decisions at all—a real decision makes one humble, one knows that it is at the mercy of more things than can be named—but elaborate systems of evasion, of illusion, designed to make the world appear to be what they and the world are not. (30)

In his essay on "the divided mind of James Baldwin," C.W.E. Bigsby comments about Baldwin's suggestion that "the root function of language is to control the universe by describing it." Bigsby claims that "the black finds that access to language is not access to power, to control over his environment and himself. Language becomes dysfunctional" (119). Although it seems clear that Baldwin would not necessarily see language as realistically "dysfunctional" as Bigsby, David seems to have given in to this dysfunctionality. He states that in his system of evasion, he is not out to look at the universe, much less to control it by describing it. For David, his problem identifying himself as a man is a sign of a dysfunctionality of language, for the language of his past, and of the dominant discourse of his present, doesn't include terms which define him. Language is heavily invested with ideological and discursive norms (sexist and homophobic forms of containment), so it isn't surprising that in attempting to define himself, David experiences many instances in which he is inarticulate about defining himself, and too frustrated by the social pressures (life in the closet) to risk otherwise. For his national identity he "resents" being called an American "because it seemed to make me nothing more than that, whatever that was; and I resented being called *not* an American because it seemed to make me nothing" (117). As for his gendered sense of identity, he experiences similar inarticulateness toward his landlord who, in taking an inventory of David's and Hella's rental home, takes a similar inventory of David's life with pointed questions about the possibilities of his growth into a "healthy manhood." David feels that in not living up to a manly "norm," he is guilty of a crime, one he should confess to the landlord, but, he claims, "I do not know how to state my crime" (95).

Eve Kosofsky Sedgwick, in her book, *Epistomology of the Closet*, refers to such "elaborate systems of evasion" as "closetedness": "a performance initiated as such by the speech act of silence" (3). According to Sedgwick, "closetedness" is a state in which discourse is contained— hence David's inarticulateness. And with the containment of discourse is the containment of David's subjectivity and desire—hence his comfort in remaining ambiguous about self-definition.

Sedgwick writes that the introduction of the term "homosexual" into Euro-American discourse in the late nineteenth century brought on "world-mapping by which every given person . . . was now considered necessarily assignable to homo- or hetero-sexuality, a binarized identity that was full of implications. . . . It was this new development that left *no space* in the culture exempt from the potent incoherences of homo/heterosexual definition" (2; italics mine). Giovanni's final pronouncement of David as "neither man nor woman, nothing that I can know or touch" (184), may confirm that David is lost in the lack of "discursive space," what Sedgwick calls "the closet," what Baldwin calls "the void." His sexual identity seems to be enclosed by the terminology of dominant discourse, and, in effect, keeps David "in the closet."

Along with David, his fiancee, Hella, experiences similar problems in self-definition. Hella, after "searching for herself" in Spain, comes back to David wishing to abandon her earlier hopes of living a life as an "independent" woman for a life as a "real" woman, married to David, having his babies. As her image of a "real woman" suggests, her identity as a woman is much dependent on David's living out a "manly" life according to the "ideology of familialism" so dominant in 1950s America (the same ideology driving "the baby boom"). Her wish to be empowered by "domestic versions of containment" includes David's being an active participant in discourse, not being passively resistant to it. As Hella packs to leave David for good, she lectures him about his failure as a man being intimately woven with his failure to be articulate:

> "I had the *right* to expect to hear from you—women are always waiting for the *man* to speak. Or hadn't you heard?" I said nothing. (217)

In response to Hella's lecturing, David is left inarticulate and feeling much less than a man:

> I stood in the doorway, watching her. I stood there in the way a small boy who has wet his pants stands before his teacher. All the words I wanted to say closed my throat, like weeds, and stopped my mouth. (216)

Although David realizes his inability to be the man Hella wants him to be, he is also left inarticulate about the type of identity he would achieve being homosexual. In fact, the term *homosexual* is never used in the novel. The language overpowering David is heterosexually inscribed and works to "closet" such terms. When trying to describe his homosexual arrangement with Giovanni, David is at a loss for words: "People have very dirty words for—for this situation" (107). And in first realizing his homosexual drive after his affair with Joey, David's attempt to describe the situation, perhaps to gain some control of it, leaves him in another space where desire and language are incommensurate: "A cavern opened in my mind, black, full of rumor, suggestion, of half-heard, half-forgotten, half-understood stories, full of dirty words. I thought I saw my future in that cavern" (15). While David finds much that is mysterious about this future, his greatest fear is that this cavern—or closet—would be the place "in which I would lose my manhood" (15). The cavern represents the discursive nature of the problem facing David: it represents a void of language in which David is left powerless and undefined, outside of any discourse he can control. And he fears a loneliness of not being "moored" to a discursive structure of "binarized identity" in which all can be defined. His problem with *les folles* exemplifies this concern: "I always found it difficult to believe that they ever went to bed with anybody, for a man who wanted a woman would certainly have rather had a real one and a man who wanted a man would certainly not want one of *them*" (38). For David, *les folles* remain outside of representation—he has no term to describe *them* either, and like his anxiety about his own undefinabilty, their "utter grotesqueness [makes him] uneasy" (39).

A problem at the center of David's attempts to reach a stable sense of self-identity is the ambiguity surrounding the "nature," or lack thereof, of his homosexuality. David seems to be struggling to find and accept his "natural" self, but, as Baldwin maintains in "The Male Prison," "the argument . . . as to whether or not homosexuality is natural seems to me completely pointless—pointless because I do not see what difference the answer makes. It seems clear, in any case, . . . the answer can never be Yes. And one of the reasons for this is that it would rob the normal—who are simply the many—of their necessary sense of security and order" (157). It seems David's attempts to be more in touch with his unnameable desires have much more to do with cultural influence than "nature." David implies that his homosexual relationship with Giovanni is the "sum," the *being* of him: "With everything in me screaming No! yet the sum of me sighed Yes" (87). Yet, he uses similar language to describe his heterosexual relationship with Hella: "I was thinking, no doubt, of our nights in bed, of the peculiar innocence and confidence, which will never come again, which had made those nights so delightful, so unrelated to the past, or to anything to come . . ." (9). Although this reflection lacks the anguish and intensity of his relationship with Giovanni, both of these reflections point to the ambiguity surrounding the "nature" of sexuality in *Giovanni's Room.*

Baldwin shows much evidence throughout the novel that there is "no space" for sexuality that is free of cultural influence. The physical spaces in which David expresses his sexuality are all transgressed by a policing eye. In reflecting on the fear that suddenly took hold of him after his night with Joey, David remarks that he wondered what Joey's mother would say when she saw the sheets. The space he finds for Hella and himself in the south of France is examined and inventoried by the landlord who is very much concerned with David's sexual relationships. And even Giovanni's room includes a wall mural of a man and woman walking together among roses, a sign that even in this place where David is supposedly most free to express his natural self, the heterosexual regime is still marked. The transgression of dominant heterosexual ideology upon these physical spaces mirrors such transgression upon what C.W.E. Bigsby would call David's "psychic territory," which has full responsibility for dictating the innocence or guilt, the purity or filth, of his sexual self.

Baldwin also allows the possibility of what comes across vaguely as self-determinism as an option for David:

... if you think of them as dirty, then they *will* be dirty—they will be dirty because you will be giving nothing, you will be despising your flesh and his. But you can make your time together anything but dirty; you can give each other something which will make both of you better—forever—if you will not be ashamed, if you will *not* play it safe. (77)

But although Jacques lectures David that the "nature" of David's sexuality has only to do with the power of his will, Baldwin gives no evidence that such will power works to create new realities. Bigsby writes that in Baldwin's work as a whole...

will . . . becomes a force with the power, if not to overcome realities, then to forge other alliances than those sanctioned by history and power. But this is not quite the confident self of the transcendentalists. In each of his books self-analysis is not only provoked by pain; it is the source of pain. Society's power is scarcely diminished. The most that the individual can hope for is to win a small psychic territory within which the harsh pragmatics of the public world no longer operate. (118-119)

In *Giovanni's Room*, "society's power is scarcely diminished," if it is diminished at all. Jacques is certainly unable to "overcome realities" as his life is marked by meaningless, purchased relationships with younger men; relationships which, from David's point of view, seem to lead only to Jacques' loneliness and abuse. And Giovanni's romantic aspirations to overcome social boundaries by literally "breaking through walls" to "make room" for himself and David, of course, prove futile as well. With these events in mind, even the achievement of "small psychic territories" seems especially difficult.

If *Giovanni's Room* does not "insist," as does *Native Son*, "that it is [social] categorization alone which is real and which cannot be transcended," Baldwin remains ambiguous, at best, about the shape transcendence takes. David writes that the "key to [his] salvation . . . is hidden in [his] flesh"; and while he does leave for Paris in the "awakening sky" of a new day, "the morning weighs on [his] shoulders with the dreadful weight of hope"(224). And in David's reflections after the course of events of the novel, he notes that "I may be drunk by morning but that will not do any good, I shall take the train to Paris anyway. The train will be the same, the people, struggling for comfort and, even, dignity on the straight-backed, wooden, third-class seats will be the same, and I will be the same"(7). Baldwin gives little, if any, indication that David has found a new discursive space for himself. The fact that the novel ends with David in motion suggests that he remains "in a constant state of motion" still pursuing "elaborate systems of evasion"—still closeted.

As for Giovanni, Baldwin doesn't provide much evidence that this is a character who has transcended the social determinism which overcomes Bigger Thomas. In fact, as Horace A. Porter writes in *Stealing the Fire*, "Baldwin . . . smuggles into *Giovanni's Room*, a place where we least expect them, *Native Son's* central themes, images and symbols"(151). Porter asserts that Baldwin sets up Giovanni as a Bigger Thomas prototype in his attempt to correct what he considers the technical failure of *Native Son*, the "tragedy" of accepting "a theology that denies him life"(151). But one has to question if any new "theology" is created. And although Porter claims otherwise, his observations suggest little difference in results:

> David concludes, 'And Giovanni fell back into the room, the streets, the world, into the presence and shadow of death.' David's focus on 'the room' and 'the presence and shadow of death' constitutes a subtle transformation of Wright's handling of the moment in *Native Son*. As Wright describes Bigger's situation: 'The reality of the room fell from him; the vast city of white people that sprawled outside took its place.' The distinctive difference reveals two points of view. (151)

Porter's comments here don't quite add up, for although David focuses on the room and Wright focuses on what is "outside" of the room, both David and Bigger remain trapped—whether it be by physical or social structures. And Baldwin's conclusion, even with the nuances Porter presents, suggests an even greater insistence by Baldwin that social categorization cannot be transcended.

C.W.E. Bigsby's statement that "the most that the individual can hope for is to win a small psychic territory within which the harsh pragmatics of the public world no longer operate" seems to hold true for *Giovanni's Room*. The statement is significant for how it speaks to David's attempt to author his own identity and for how it speaks to Baldwin's own attempt to make a "discursive territory" for himself in the public domain. David's decisions to move geographically, from America to Paris and from Paris to the French countryside, reflect his need to move into new "psychic territory" where he can construct a new discursive space for himself with "elaborate systems of evasion," bound together with "legend, myth, coercion." While, as I've noted earlier, the ending of the novel leaves readers with little more than ambivalence about David's possibilities for transcending the "unprecedented level of social control" of the "domestic versions of containment" of the 1950s, it also leaves his *desire* to do so in question. David has presented no evidence in his confessions that he has found the possibility of finding a "place" for his "natural" self to exist comfortably, nor is he completely convinced that a "natural" self even exists.

David's ambivalence about the confinement of social language structures is compounded by a similar ambivalence of the structure of his confessional narrative itself which, on the one hand, depicts homoerotic love positively, associating it with the innocent expression of love and with healing power, yet, on the other hand, depicts it negatively with the implication that both David and Giovanni are sexual deviants produced by depraved psychological and socioeconomic circumstances. James Levin, in his study of *The Gay Novel in America* places such depictions in the context of what he calls the "Freudian fifties": "A clear decline in tolerance toward homosexuality occurred and popular social science theories were enlisted to justify more conservative points of view"(109). Levin writes that *Giovanni's Room* "manages to avoid the usual notion of Freudian causality" (144), but the novel does record David's troublesome childhood with typical Freudian dysfunctions including his abusive father and lack of mother. And a similar troublesome history is given of Giovanni's past heterosexual relationship producing a still-born child. Both histories suggest that their homosexuality is the "misplacement" of their sexual selves.

Yasmin Y. DeGout asserts that Baldwin's duality—between representing homosexuality as innocent and natural and representing it as "misplaced" and deviant—stems from the acknowledged influence of "differing value systems of mainstream America and of the homoerotic community . . . upon his perception of homoerotic love. . . . The reader, like Baldwin, is forced to oscillate between two irreconcilable interpretations of the nature of homosexuality" (426). DeGout maintains that such ambiguity "has allowed readers to approach the work in a way that way suits their own psychological needs or value systems"(435). Likewise, it is this ambiguity which is the site and substance of David's construction—or the evasion thereof—of his manhood to suit his own immediate psychological needs. The cost for David, however, is the absence of any sustained commitment in any loving relationship. David's solution to the limitations of placement is always to continue moving—to stay closeted—and to allow ambiguity to replace commitment and the risks that go along with it.

Giovanni's Room, because of its theme of the complexities of constructing manhood and its questioning of the limits of self-determination, reflects the existence of similar issues shaping the identity of Baldwin himself at the time it was published. Baldwin writes in "Everybody's Protest Novel" that "In overlooking, denying, and evading [Bigger's] complexity—which is nothing more than the disquieting complexity of ourselves—we are diminished and we perish; only within this web of ambiguity, paradox, this hunger, danger, darkness, can we find at once ourselves and the power to free us from ourselves" (15). Unlike David who is endlessly overlooking, denying, and evading his complexity, Baldwin risks the safety of the norms of mainstream publishing with the publication of *Giovanni's Room*. While many critics found heroic Baldwin's move away from what Leslie Fiedler calls "the Negro writer's usual obsession with his situation as a Negro in a white culture, an obsession which keeps him forever writing the first book"(146-7), many thought this move too risky. Dial Press, who published the work after Knopf turned it down, had a great deal to lose by publishing a novel about homosexuality by a little known author, black or white, in 1956. And their decision to exclude Baldwin's photograph from the text suggests that part of their fear was in having a black man associated with an "all-white" novel—especially one about homosexuality (Campbell 106). The rejection of Baldwin by Eldridge Cleaver in *Soul on Ice* is an example of the hostile reaction such a move could produce from Baldwin's black audience:

> In this land of dichotomies and disunited opposites, those truly concerned with the resurrection of black Americans have had eternally to deal with black intellectuals who have become their own opposites, taking on all the behavior patterns of the enemy, vices and virtue, in an effort to aspire to alien standards in all respects. . . . The black homosexual, when his twist has a racial nexus, is an extreme embodiment of this contradiction. The white man has deprived him of his masculinity, castrated him from the center of his burning skull. . . . (100-101)

In effect, Cleaver is accusing Baldwin of being an Uncle Tom for much the same reason that Uncle Tom himself took on such a "negative" reputation: both refused a violent, angry reaction to white culture (that of Bigger Thomas), a reaction which many blacks felt defined their "manhood." Cleaver's remarks show a direct correlation between an unquestioned heterosexual masculinity and a strong sense of racial identity.

In the writing of *Giovanni's Room*, Baldwin does "create a discursive space" for (at least) himself as a black homosexual artist, but it is important to realize that this space is one which could have alienated him from an Afro-American culture that may not have been willing to negotiate its sense of manhood. Furthermore, it could have had the same response from a white culture which, to a great extent, fed its own sense of masculine domination by viewing black men as having an uncontrollable animalistic (hetero)sexual potency. Perhaps these overwhelming ideological pressures bring Baldwin to conclude that including homosexuality, the "Negro problem," and a Paris setting in the same novel "would have been quite beyond my powers" (Weatherby 125).

Cleaver's reaction is also significant for its raising of the issue of America as the "land of dichotomies and disunited opposites." Unlike David who recognizes only the extreme dichotomies produced by social ideology, between clean heterosexuality and dirty homosexuality for instance, Baldwin recognizes options beyond "dichotomies and disunited opposites." His pursuit of other discursive spaces reflects his reinterpretation of W.E.B. DuBois' notion of double-consciousness to include not only the "second-sight" that the construction of race has created, but also the "second-sight" (third-sight?) that gender construction creates. In striving for new space to define himself, Baldwin sees himself as existing in an even greater complexity than Dubois' "twoness." With *Giovanni's Room* Baldwin reconfigures the Duboisian notion of "two unreconciled strivings; two warring ideals in one dark body, whose dogged strength alone keeps it from being torn asunder"(3). Baldwin sees his own "significant living" lying outside of binary structures and their exclusions, but, unlike his protagonist, he overcomes fear and "closetedness," and in doing so he opens new discursive space for black homosexual manhood.

CHAPTER 2

Alice Walker:
Finding Discursive Space
in the Aesthetic Realm
The Third Life of Grange Copeland

> As long as black people foolishly cling to the
> rather politically naive and dangerous assump-
> tion that it is in the interests of black liberation
> to support sexism and male domination, all on
> efforts to decolonize our minds and transform
> society will fall.
>
> —BELL HOOKS,
> "RECONSTRUCTING BLACK MASCULINITY"

> there is no fixed place
> on earth for man
> or woman.
> —ALICE WALKER, *REVOLUTIONARY PETUNIAS*

Much of Alice Walker's fiction, and especially her novels *The Third Life of Grange Copeland* and *The Color Purple*, address issues concerning the construction of manhood and the significance of such social construction on the lives of black woman. The Third Life of Grange Copeland, Walker's first novel, published in 1970, is perhaps her most substantial statement about manhood in that the central issue confronting the novel's protagonist is the transformation from his being an abusive husband and father to being a wanderer and petty thief in Harlem to his "third life" as a responsible and nurturing grandfather to his granddaughter Ruth. For Walker and for other black women novelists of the twentieth century, including Zora Neale Hurston, Ann Petry, Toni Morrison, and Gloria Naylor, the future of black women's empowerment has much to do with the control of white and largely racist definitions of black manhood.

The fiction of Walker and her contemporaries, including Morrison and Naylor, takes shape largely as a response to gender construction as it is presented by the more influential male Afro-American voices of the previous generation, especially Richard Wright, James Baldwin, Ralph Ellison, Malcolm X, and Eldridge Cleaver. In a recent *New York Times Magazine* interview, Toni Morrison's comments address this influence. Morrison writes that although James Baldwin's writing was one of the most important influences on her work, in her novels there is a conscious attempt made to marginalize dominant notions of manhood as they are dictated by white patriarchy, a strategy she doesn't find in the work of Black men:

> This kind of ground shifting seems much more common to black women writers. Not so much to black men writers. Black men writers are often interested in their relation with white men. White men, by and large, are not powerful figures in black women's literature. . . . When I began, there was just one thing I wanted to write about, which was the devastation of racism on the most vulnerable, the most helpless unit in society—a black female and a child. I wanted to write about what it was like to be the subject of racism. (74)

Morrison's remarks suggest that the preoccupation of black male writers with finding legitimacy for themselves as men didn't change much about representations of black women who have remained effectively marginalized in their works. Calvin Hernton, author *of The Sexual Mountain and Black Women Writers*, writes that this problem has been present throughout the history of Afro-American writing:

> Historically the battle line of racial struggle in the United States has been drawn exclusively as a struggle between the men of the races. Everything having to do with the race has been defined and counter-defined by the men as a question of whether black people were or were not a race of Men. The central concept and the universal metaphor around which all aspects of the racial situation revolve is 'Manhood.' (38)

To exemplify some of this problem, Wright's *Native Son* is again a significant text. Even with Wright's reminder to readers that "throughout [*Native Son*] there is but one point of view: Bigger's" (xxxii), both black and white reviews and critiques of the work have taken Bigger's experience to be symbolic of "the black experience" in the United States. Only since the widespread ascendancy of feminist and gender criticism have critics noticed significant problems with such a "universalist" take on the work—especially in consideration of Bigger's fight to "achieve a sense of manhood." In an important feminist rereading of *Native Son*, published as recently as 1988 by *Modern Fiction Studies*, Alan W. France notes that earlier feminist readings of *Native Son* have found it easy to excuse blatantly misogynistic characterizations of women because, as Wright has insisted in his introduction to the work, "this is Bigger's story." France writes that

> . . . it is time now to revoke these privileges accorded to Bigger and to recover the radical alterity in the text that reduces women to property, valuable only to the extent they serve as objects of phallocentric status conflicts. If read as the negative polarity of the text, this process of male reification and appropriation pervades the work. (152)

France's point is exemplified most clearly in the passages of *Native Son* in which Bigger is most aware of his identity as manly. At such points the results are harsh for women:

> The knowledge that he had killed a white girl they loved and regarded as a symbol of their beauty made him feel the equal to them, like a man who had been somehow cheated, but had now evened the score. (155)

The writing of "manhood" as somehow being produced through rape is also a part of "Bigger's story" in *Native Son*. In Wright's narration of the scene in which Bigger rapes and murders Bessie, the narrative strategy of the scene is primarily focused on examining what this rape means to Bigger. This scene, like much if not all of *Native Son*, focuses on Bigger's inner turmoil as he feels forced to this action because of feelings of entrapment. Although Bessie is the victim in this scene, the writing of the scene suggests that the primary issue is Bigger's victimization of which the rape and murder of Bessie are only a part.

In *The Third Life of Grange Copeland*, Alice Walker undertakes a "rewriting," to use Linda Abbandonato's term, of black male narratives of victimization. Abbandonato, in her essay on "Rewriting the Heroine's Story in *The Color Purple*," writes that "the challenge facing feminists is no less than to 'rewrite cultural narratives, and to define the terms of another perspective—a view from elsewhere'" (298). Although Abbandonato is addressing the role of Celie in *The Color Purple*, similar issues about reinscription are central in *The Third Life of Grange Copeland* as well. In fact, *The Third Life of Grange Copeland* sets the stage for *The Color Purple* in that it exposes the nature of the gender problems Walker goes about remedying in utopic fashion in the latter novel. Abbandonato writes that in *The Color Purple* "Celie's burden in building a self on a site of negation is shared by any woman who attempts to establish an identity outside of patriarchal definition. . . . But it is no easy task for women to authorize themselves as women, to disengage their feminine identity from the ideological master narratives that inscribe it" (298). What Abbandonato sees as Celie's burden in *The Color Purple*, I propose, is precisely the burden Grange Copeland carries in this earlier novel. With *The Third Life of Grange Copeland*, Alice Walker addresses black masculinity especially as it has been inscribed by such cultural narratives as Richard Wright's *Native Son*. Grange Copeland and his son Brownfield are trapped in similar harsh circumstances as Bigger Thomas, and both take out their victimization on women in attempts to regain some sense of manhood. Grange's change is produced through his ability to redefine what it means to be a black man, and it is "no easy task" for him to construct a positive sense of masculine identity from the ideological master narratives of a white racist patriarchy which positions black men "on a site of negation."

   In *The Third Life of Grange Copeland* Walker investigates the possibilities for new discursive spaces for black men to be defined—and with this, new ways for understanding gender identity as a whole, for men and for women. Central to Walker's feminist agenda in this novel is the (lack of) fixity concerning definitions of manhood. And similar to James Baldwin's narrative strategy in *Giovanni's Room*, Walker's approach to "manhood" is one in which both physical and discursive spaces bear great metaphorical significance. From the very opening sentence of the novel, in which Brownfield is not able to keep "his eyes off the back of the receding automobile," the issue of Grange's and Brownfield's entrapment is present. The living quarters of black sharecroppers become an emblem of crushing degradation and hopelessness:

> Brownfield turned from watching the road and looked with hateful scrutiny at the house they lived in. It was a cabin of two rooms with a chimney at one end. The roof was of rotting grey shingles; the sides of the house were grey vertical slabs; the whole aspect of the house grey. It was lower in the middle than at its ends, and resembled a sway-backed animal put out to pasture. A stone-based well sat functionally in the middle of the yard, its mossy wooden bucket dangling above it

by some rusty chain and frazzled lengths of rope. Where water was dashed behind the well, wild morning-glories bloomed, their tendrils reaching as far as the woodpile, which was a litter of tree trunks, slivers of carcass bones deposited by the dog and discarded braces and bits that had pained the jaws and teeth of many a hard-driven mule. (16)

The repeated images of decay and privation work to contextualize the experience of this southern sharecropping family with symbolic reminders of failure and mortality (Mason 298). Walker juxtaposes this description of the cabin with the novel's first description of Grange:

> He was thirty-five but seemed much older. His face and eyes had a dispassionate vacancy and sadness, as if a great fire had been extinguished within him and was just recently missed. He seemed devoid of any emotion, while Brownfield watched him, except that of bewilderment. A bewilderment so complete he did not really appear to know what he saw, although his hand continued to gesture, more or less aimlessly, and his lips moved, shaping unintelligible words. While his son watched, Grange lifted his shoulders and let them fall. Brownfield knew this movement well; it was a fatal shrug. It meant that his father saw nothing about the house that he could change and would therefore give up gesturing about it and he would never again think of repairing it. (17)

Several important themes concerning the fixity of Grange's physical and discursive placement come into play in the early juxtaposition of these two passages. First, the identities of Grange and Brownfield are developed "on the site of negation." As Brownfield laments that his family does not possess the great symbol of his uncle's freedom, an automobile, the cabin they live in and Grange himself are noteworthy more for what they lack than for what they possess. The house is grey, a symbol of rot, decay, and lifelessness; and Grange has a "dispassionate vacancy," "devoid of emotion," inarticulate, unintelligible, and aimless.

Second, Walker makes it clear that the "site of negation" transcends the physicality of the scene. In his analysis of Walker's initial description of Grange, Theodore Mason notes that

> Grange's sole response to this complete deprivation can only be 'the fatal shrug.' Revealing here is Walker's use of absence as a profound signifier. Literally, there is *nothing* to Grange's life, so that he may rec-

ognize himself and his family merely as experiencing the inversion of
what other people (mostly white) have. His life is so debilitating and
lacking of substance that it propels him beyond speech for its expression. The shrug itself expresses another level of absence by communicating that no remedy exists that might relieve the persistent
nothingness and vacancy. (299)

The fact that Grange can only shrug signifies that he is outside of language and the power it provides for self-definition. In this respect Grange
is similar to all of the protagonists of this study. As both Wright's Bigger
and Baldwin's David are unable to be articulate, Grange is depicted as
being "on a site of negation" in terms of language. The physical "space"
of his cabin is symbolic of the negative discursive "space" Grange holds
in the dominant discourse of society. Change and repair are notions he is
unable to articulate; he has no authorial capacity, and his discursive
space is one of "nothingness and vacancy," in actuality a discursive
silence that leaves him powerless to "rewrite" his social and personal
identity.

The fact that "Brownfield knew the movement well," referring to
"the fatal shrug," is another important feature of these passages. Walker
provides other scenes as well, especially with the white landowner, Ship-
ley, in which Grange's inarticulateness is witnessed by Brownfield; in effect, the permanence of Grange's incapacity to rewrite himself is
transmitted to Brownfield's generation. All Brownfield learns is to
revoice (or to "re-silence") what he has witnessed, which are, in Mason's
words, "fictions whose primary theme involves dominance and oppression and whose primary trope is enclosure" (302).

The significance given to the control of language as the key to self-
redefinition is best played out in Mem, Brownfield's wife and the mother
of his children. Mem's capacity to be articulate—she is a teacher of En-
glish—distinguishes her from every other character of the novel. She attempts to create a new discursive paradigm for her family to live by,
including her demands for the proper language Brownfield should use,
and the proper way she should be addressed. But as Mem's health fails
her, Brownfield's drive toward the oppressive dominance by which he
has learned to live leaves Mem discursively powerless and literally inarticulate:

The starch of her speech simply went out of her and what came out of
her mouth sagged, just as what had come out of her ancestors sagged.

Except that where their speech had been beautiful because it was all they knew and a part of them without thinking about it, hers came out flat and ugly, like a tongue broken and trying to mend itself from desperation. (82)

Walker notes that "for a woman like Mem, who had barely escaped the culture of poverty, a slip back into that culture was the easiest thing in the world" (81). Ultimately she is even forced to burn her books, the material signs of her literacy, simply to survive in the environment of Brownfield's oppression.

Through this battle between Mem and Brownfield, Walker provides a great deal of reinforcement to the connection she develops between control of language and its importance in being identified as manly. At the height of her power over Brownfield, Mem takes over the masculine role of being the active controller of discourse and of the place (physical and discursive) to which they will move. She dictates this new discourse from behind the barrel of a rifle, "controlling the cool hard gun barrel down between his thighs." The phallic symbolism on Walker's part is almost too obvious. And ultimately both characters experience name changes as she insists on being called "Mem, Mrs. Copeland, or Mrs. Mem R. Copeland," and she completes the "unmanning" of Brownfield by addressing him as "boy." Her discursive power allows her to effectively redefine herself and Brownfield—at least temporarily.

The connection between discourse and placement is explored further during the "third life" of Grange after he has bought a farm, his refuge, which he fences off from the rest of society. The farm becomes a significant place in the novel, for it represents enclosure as affirmative and empowering. It is in this place, where Grange effectively separates himself from his past obsession with authoritarial control of the white world around him, that Grange begins to show his empowerment discursively. While he, Josie, and Ruth prepare ambrosia in preparation for Christmas (because that is "what all the gods used to eat before there just came to be one God"), Grange begins to practice his talent for storytelling:

Grange would stop ten or fifteen times during the process to tell a story, or the truth about someone or somebody. He knew all the Uncle Remus stories by heart, although he could make up better ones about a smart plantation man named John. John became Ruth's hero because he could talk himself out of any situation and reminded her of Grange. (183)

Grange takes on a godlike identity in this passage, and with it, the ability to create his own discursive base of self-affirmation. Grange now is able to rewrite his identity because he has the godlike power to determine his own truth, and to create his own heroes who are, of course, reflections of himself.

It is worth noting that in an earlier reference to God in the novel, when Mem tells Brownfield to "call on the one you serves," Brownfield thinks "irresistibly" of Captain Davis: "the tall old cracker just popped into his mind like he was God or somebody"(134). This is a message Walker articulates more fully in Shug's advice to Celie about her similar relationship to "godlike" male discursive control in *The Color Purple*:

> . . . You have to git man off your eyeball, before you can see anything
> a'tall. Man corrupt everything, say Shug. He on your box of grits, in
> your head and all over the radio. He try to make you think he every-
> where. Soon as you think he everywhere, you think he God. But he
> ain't. Whenever you trying to pray, a man plot himself on the other end
> of it, tell him to git lost, say Shug. (179)

Grange "gits" the white man "off his eyeball." In Grange's earlier lives, including the life Brownfield never transcends, white men have the power of God, the discursive power to determine truth and to create a mythology by which all its believers gain their sense of identity. With this in mind, it is no coincidence that the most impressive feature of Grange and Ruth's hero is his ability to "talk himself out of any situation." Again, Walker's message is that controlling discursive power is the key to the freedom required to redefine oneself.

The other stories Grange tells shows the extent to which Grange's control of language is truly a subversive act. Linda Abbandonato's feminist theorizing about *The Color Purple* again provides some interesting perspective in terms of Grange. In reflecting on the subversive quality of Celie's role in that novel, she quotes Luce Irigaray's point that "if [women] keep on speaking the same language together, [they're] going to reproduce the same history. Begin the same stories all over again" (298). In his attempt to stop reproducing the same history, a problem he sees that he has already contributed to in his influence on Brownfield, Grange becomes actively involved in telling new kinds of stories. These stories contain interesting trickster figures, "about two-heads and conjurers, men and women more sensitive than the average spook"(183). Also included in his stories is the story of "how he came to join the church."

But instead of the expected tale of piety and solemnity, Grange's story is a humorous tale about his deal with God to have his Uncle Buster swallow a fly, the result of which is his moral about why he doesn't believe in God and other "conventional absurdities" he and Ruth see in organized religion: " . . . it was funny, what they witnessed every Sunday—the placid, Christ-deferential self-righteousness of men who tortured their children and on Saturday nights beat their wives"(188). Grange's new narrative foundation extends even to his containing the "discursive space" of television and the white mythology it mediates. In response to Ruth's question about why Grange can't fight racism the way Wyatt Earp guns down outlaws, Grange responds that there are "too many in real life." The way Grange goes about controlling and subverting traditional narratives with his own, somewhat radical folk narratives shows how Grange's path toward changing the meaning of his manhood is truly an act based on the subversion of language itself.

In juxtaposition to Grange's freeing use of language, Walker symbolically connects Brownfield's lack of freedom to the way white discourse contains him. After learning to read and write while in prison, Brownfield reflects with another inmate about how his situation is similar to that of the words in a newspaper:

> "I felt just like the words here in the newspaper must feel, all printed up. The line already decided. No moving to the left or to the right, like a mule wearing blinders. These words just run one word right behind the other to the end of the page." . . . "Just think how this word here'd feel if it could move right out of this line and set itself down over here!" The two men pondered the power of the mobile, self-determined word. . . . " . . . you'd think more people would think about how they ain't got no more say about what goes on with 'em than a pair of shoes or a little black piece of writing in a newspaper that can't move no matter what it stands for. How come we the only ones that knowed we was men?" Leaning heavily on his pencil Brownfield wrote m-e-n, then waited for the word to rise and beat its chest. (235)

Unlike Grange's "godlike" use of language, the key associations linking Brownfield to language are animalistic, like a mule or some kind of ape. In a significant distinction between Mem's discursive control over Brownfield reducing him to the status of "boy," still human but immature, the discursive control of white patriarchy provides the ideology necessary to cause Brownfield to come to define even his "manhood" as ironically, something less than human. Brownfield does write the word m-e-n as an attempt to take some kind of discursive control over his identity, but his attempt takes place in an imprisoning space of white patriarchy—the prison cell. Of course, the newspaper, containing the language and ideology of the white racist society around him, is also a "prison house of language" from Brownfield's point of view. For him "the word" is far more likely to lead to his imprisonment in white discourse than to self-determination.

With all of the enclosing spaces in this novel, both physical and discursive, the space of Grange's farm is perhaps most significant for it is the enclosure in which change is allowed to occur. While the farm has the utilitarian purpose of providing safety for Grange and Ruth, this space is more important for its mythic qualities: in it the confines of discursive and physical enclosure seem to be breached. In his essay on the dynamics of enclosure in *The Third Life of Grange Copeland*, Theodore Mason writes that

> The farm is clearly a physical space, but even more importantly an analogue for imaginative space, a way of "reading" and constructing the world. This construction of reality depends upon a recognition of others and a humane open-mindedness. (305)

Perhaps the most important spatial element of the farm is the unlimited sense of freedom it helps to foster in the hope for Ruth's future. When Ruth asks Grange about her future, Grange's first response is to have her stay on the farm "till kingdom come," but, as Robert Butler points out, "Ruth immediately rejects such a static conception of her future, telling him 'I'm not going to be a hermit.' The same fences which give him a sense of security eventually induce claustrophobia in her. She needs unlimited space if she is to fulfill the deepest promptings of her ever-growing self" (73). Unlike Brownfield who is content with the first life of his father, Ruth rejects the lifestyle of her father, rejecting with it the traditional and oppressive notions of gender it carries. Grange fosters Ruth's desire to change places, encouraging her to go away from Baker county to college and delighting in "examining maps, wondering about the places in the world he would never see"(214). Grange also delights in telling Ruth the story of Exodus as part of his giving her a sense of indeterminate vision toward a mythic promised land. And, moreover, Grange's openness to a mythic promised land is further signified in the opening of his farm's physical boundaries to the white activists Ruth befriends, Helen and Quincy. His desire to protect them despite his doubts that they can achieve their goals shows his openness to their dreams of bringing about significant change.

It is important to recognize that the enclosed space of the farm doesn't necessarily change the oppressive social reality outside the farm. Grange notes after his transformation that "the white folks hated me and I hated myself until I started hating them in return and loving myself. Then I tried just loving me and then you, and ignoring them as much as I could" (273). Although Grange is able, in his third life, to construct a community outside the social structure which "posits definitions of manhood and responsibility which the black man does not have the opportunity to attain" (Hogue 106), this resolution is based largely on his ability to ignore oppressive social structures, not change them. The construction of the freeing discursive space of the farm is problematized by the social realities that helped construct it, the most obvious of which are the events surrounding the moment of transformation in Grange's life.

In a reproduction of the moment of change in Wright's *Native Son*, when Bigger Thomas gains a psychological sense of manhood and freedom from his accidentally killing Mary Dalton, Walker has Grange's transformation to his new sense of manhood occur upon the death of a white woman:

> Her contempt for him had been the last straw; never again would he care what happened to any of them. She was perhaps the only one of them he would ever sentence to death. He had killed a thousand, ten thousand, a whole country of them in his mind. She was the first, and would probably be the only real one. The death of the woman was simply murder, he thought, and soul condemning; but in a strange way, a bizarre way, it liberated him. . . . It was the taking of the white woman's life. . . . that forced him to want to try to live again. He believed that, against his will, he had stumbled on the necessary act that black men must commit to regain, or to manufacture their manhood, their self-respect. They must kill their oppressors.(218)

This scene places a problematic contradiction at the center of Walker's message about discursive reinscription. As noted above, the scene *reproduces* Bigger Thomas, it doesn't "rewrite" him. Obviously, the formula Grange uses to "manufacture" his manhood is undercut by the fact that it is the same formula Brownfield uses in manufacturing his manhood as he kills the person whom he determines to be his oppressor, Mem.

Other problematic factors also contribute to the construction of Grange's third life and to the new possibilities given to Ruth. First, Grange doesn't love Josie, but he takes advantage of her for her money to buy the farm. Second, ultimate protection from Brownfield isn't brought about though any new life for him. Instead, for Ruth to be free Brownfield must be murdered, and Grange subsequently killed as well. Although a new discursive space is constructed which holds great hope for a more positive future, the foundation for that space is made up of similar violence and victimization of women to that which it was meant to overcome. W. Lawrence Hogue sees such contradictions in light of the unresolved social reality the text is forced to live with:

> . . . we see how *The Third Life* constitutes what Frederic Jameson calls a 'symbolic act' whereby 'real social contradictions, insurmountable in their own terms, find a purely formal resolution in the aesthetic realm.' The oppressive, violent white male who causes the black male to be subservient and powerless is still unresolved in the social real. This explains why *The Third Life*—by resolving in the aesthetic realm the historical oppression of black women by killing Brownfield and transforming Grange—has to exclude and distance itself from the real political and social contradiction—the oppressive white force—because it cannot directly and immediately conceptualize it. (106)

To take Hogue's statement one step further, the discursive space Grange constructs is "the aesthetic realm"—that place where he can "exclude and distance" himself from "real political and social contradiction" and where he is the master of the production of his own discourse, his own identity. Of course, the issue of liberating possibilities produced in the "aesthetic realm" reflects on Walker's novel itself, the power in Walker's "discursive space" to redefine negative identities. Like Ruth's "reading" and learning from Grange's radical discourse, Walker's construction of the fiction of the novel, her "aesthetic realm" provides a radical discourse which can affect the future.

To conclude this chapter, I wish to make the point that Walker's "rewriting black manhood" isn't necessarily based on exposing a truth that was previously hidden; instead, Walker presents the key to reinscription in ignoring old oppressive fictions, replacing them with newer, more liberating fictions. James Coleman, in his book, *Blackness and Modernism*, sees this postmodern formula for discursive liberation to be both pessimistic and optimistic: "it is more pessimistic because it views art as having no ability to change reality; it is more optimistic because it sees an opportunity for subjective fulfillment of the reader and self-fulfillment in art" (6). To a large extent, the social realities readers are left with at the end of *The Third Life of Grange Copeland* are not much more positive than those found at the end of Wright's *Native Son*. However, the hopeful possibilities produced within Grange's new discursive space are limitless. Walker makes it clear that the construction of mythic and expansive discursive spaces is the key to redefining manhood and rewriting oppressive social fictions. But she also makes it clear that new spaces for discursive and social change, like the discursive control of white patriarchal hegemony they resist, are not seamless. The paradox surrounding the making of Grange's discursive space is that the freedom derived from it is produced through what Theodore Mason calls the "recognition of the dynamic state of enclosure"(307). To be effective, his discursive space must remain enclosed, but it must also be open and expansive.

CHAPTER 3

John Edgar Wideman:
Philadelphia Fire
Fighting the Battle to Define Reality

> *To take stock, to make sense, to attempt to con-*
> *trol or write a narrative of self—how hopeless*
> *any of these tasks must seem when the* self *at-*
> *tempting this harrowing business is no more*
> *reliable than a shadow, a chimera coming and*
> *going with a will or will-lessness of its own. . . .*
> *He must learn in periods of calm, to repeat a*
> *story endlessly to himself: there is a good boy,*
> *someone who loves and is loved, who can sur-*
> *vive in spite of shifting, unstable conditions of*
> *good and evil, being and nothingness.*
> —JOHN EDGAR WIDEMAN, *PHILADELPHIA FIRE*

> *When he comments on bad news it's usually a*
> *grunt, a nod, or a gesture with his hands that*
> *says all there is to say and says, a million words*
> *wouldn't make any difference, would they.*
> —JOHN EDGAR WIDEMAN,
> *BROTHERS AND KEEPERS*

Beginning with the publication of his first novel, *A Glance Away*, written in 1967, John Edgar Wideman's career as a writer of fiction and nonfiction has been autobiographically driven, addressing issues pertinent to young black men growing up in urban America. I have chosen to include Wideman's 1990 novel, *Philadelphia Fire*, in this study because of the way it so poignantly addresses the social construction of black manhood as it relates to the control of language. *Philadelphia Fire* explores the frustration involved for black men attempting to rewrite debilitating narratives of black manhood that have led to their alienation and disempowerment.

The novel's narrator and protagonist, Cudjoe, is a black man who has returned to his old neighborhood in West Philadelphia after a ten year hiatus spent as a bartender on the Greek island of Mykonos. What draws him back to Philadelphia is the novel's central image, the 1985 firebombing of the Afro-American communal group MOVE (based on the actual event) at the behest of a Philadelphia city administration headed by a black mayor. In particular, it is a boy who escapes the fire (also part of the actual event), who sparks Cudjoe's obsession:

> The boy who is the only survivor of the holocaust on Osage Avenue, the child who is brother, son, a lost limb haunting him since he read about the fire in a magazine. He must find the child to be whole again. Cudjoe can't account for the force drawing him to the story nor why he indulges a fantasy of identification with a boy who escaped the massacre. He knows the ache of absence, the phantom presence of pain that tricks him into reaching down again and again to stroke the emptiness. He's stopped asking why. His identification with the boy persists like a discredited rumor. Like Hitler's escape from the bunker. Like the Second Coming. (8)

Cudjoe comes back to Philadelphia with the idea that he is going to write about the fire, possibly to activate the mythic potential of this boy, a new man rising phoenix-like from the fire and destruction that have left Cudjoe's old neighborhood a wasteland.

Philadelphia Fire starts out as a third-person narrative, but the novel quickly becomes a fragmented, postmodern conglomeration of first-person authorial reflections (from Cudjoe and Wideman) and surreal scenarios which reveal Cudjoe trying to piece together a positive sense of self and community from a past marked by his failures as a father, husband, teacher, and writer. In one of these reflections Wideman indicates that at the center of this "tempestuous" novel is Cudjoe's attempt at directing his middle-school students in a production of Shakespeare's *The Tempest*:

> This is the central event. I assure you. I repeat. Whatever my assurance is worth. Being the fabulator. This is the central event, this production of *The Tempest* staged by Cudjoe in the late 1960's, outdoors, in a park in West Philly. Though it comes here, wandering like a Flying Dutchman in and out of the narrative, many places at once. *The Tempest* sits dead center, the storm in the eye of the storm, figure within a figure,

play within play, it is the bounty and hub of all else written about the fire. (132)

Cudjoe's interpretation of *The Tempest* as a tale of "colonialism, imperialism, recidivism, the royal fucking over of weak by strong, colored by white, many by few"(127) makes this choice of play most appropriate as the center of such a politically charged novel. The reason Cudjoe gives to his students for rewriting and producing *The Tempest*, to "derail de tale," is at the heart of his commitment as a teacher and writer. Cudjoe is resolved throughout *Philadelphia Fire*, and especially in relation to his producing Shakespeare's play, to "derail" the discursive paradigm that leaves him blocked as a writer and as an agent of change. He wants to create a new script, a new discourse from which the next generation of Afro-Americans in his neighborhood can be unified. Although *The Tempest* is obviously not a specifically American text, it is about colonization as far as Cudjoe is concerned, and for Cudjoe, colonization is directed at culture, which at root is language. If dominant American discourses have worked only to isolate and disempower Afro-Americans, then his role as teacher is to focus on language as the tool of colonization. With this in mind, his goal is to "rewrite" the script from which they gain their identity:

> . . . one of my jobs as model and teacher is to unteach you, help you separate the good from the bad from the ugly. Specifically, in this case, to remove de tail. Derail de tale. Disembarrass, disabuse, disburden— demonstrate conclusively that Mr. Caliban's behind is clean and unencumbered, good as anybody else's. That the tail was a tale. Nothing more or less than a ill-intentioned big fat lie. (131)

Like Grange Copeland in Alice Walker's novel, Cudjoe attempts to take control of language. Grange "rewrites" folk tales and produces some of his own; likewise, Cudjoe chooses to "derail" an equally mythic text. Cudjoe envisions Shakespeare's text to be at the center of white mythology about black manhood. It both addresses and takes part in the "discursive colonization" of black men as powerless, cannibalistic (Calibanistic) subhumans, lost in and overcome by the "tempestuous" forces of white language. *The Tempest* becomes a representative focal point of white discourse leaving no place for any version of black manhood that is autonomous. But Wideman—and Cudjoe—understand *The Tempest* for its mythic significance: it is not immutable, it can be "derailed," and it remains open to refashioning by the experience and bias of the culture or individual "rewriting" it.

With *The Tempest* at its center, *Philadelphia Fire* is a novel that presents Cudjoe, like Caliban, as colonized by language, reduced to being victimized by and reactionary to it. One can imagine Cudjoe, the novelist and producer of drama, responding to America's white culture as Caliban responds to Miranda's "Abhorred Slave" speech: "You taught me language, and my profit on't / Is, I know how to curse. The red-plague rid you / For learning me your language" (I,ii,363-5). Wideman leaves evidence that cursing, which is a large part of Cudjoe's use of language, is not the creative use of language Cudjoe needs to "derail de tale." Cursing doesn't help Caliban to redefine himself; it works only to validate Prospero and Miranda's belief in his illegitimacy. Wideman's reference later in the novel to J.B., a drifter on the Philadelphia streets, unpacks the nature of this problem:

> Fuck it. Two words he usually settles for when he tries to reason why. Or why not. At least once a day he's bullied into this familiar dialogue, forced to admit that he has no life worth thinking about and forced to admit that he'll continue saying yes to it. (186)

J.B.'s curse is something he must use, not as part of his agency with language, but in reaction to the agency of others. Like Caliban he is forced to "settle" on cursing as part of his saying yes to a worthlessness inscribed by the discourses of others. Nothing about his (lack of) power over language suggests that he will be transgressive or redemptive in any vital way.

While Caliban's lead here is a part of Cudjoe's planning in his production of the play (and of the novels he tries to write), his interpretation of Caliban as desiring Miranda's flesh before her word—"Flesh today. Word Tomorrow is the proper order of business"(142)—is another telling connection to Cudjoe's character and to his failure to use language effectively. Cudjoe reflects often about his control of language being central to his empowerment, but, at the same time, he prefers flesh to words. This apparent contradiction presents one of what Jan Clausen calls "inexplicable gaps and unanswered questions" that play a huge role in Cudjoe's problematic sense of identity. Like Bigger Thomas in Wright's *Native Son*, Cudjoe often reproduces, not rewrites, the colonizing objectification by which he feels victimized. This is especially apparent in Cudjoe's voyeuristic objectification of women. Cudjoe spends a great deal of time narrating, and obsessing over, the relationship of Caliban and Miranda much as he did with the many women he has watched from afar earlier in the novel. In one of these voyeuristic episodes, he reflects upon what he likes about his "nonrelationship" with the woman he watches; his comments here seem to sum up the attitude behind his "view" of all women:

> She was close enough. Untouchable, unreachable, and that's what he liked about those hours he watched her going about her business. No name. No history. She was the body of a woman. No beginning, middle, end in her life. All woman, any woman. (54)

Cudjoe's voyeuristic objectification of this woman is duplicated in many forms throughout the novel. As Jan Clausen notes, often in these scenes Cudjoe visually fragments women (fragmentation similar to Bigger's hacking Mary Dalton to pieces), leaving an absence of whole female characters, "their place too often taken by fetishized parts, the 'dark crease . . . spray of curly hairs . . . dark hinge between her legs . . . delicate pinks, soft fleece'" (Clausen 52). Although Bigger Thomas doesn't fetishize as Cudjoe does, the actions of both characters certainly work against any commitment to wholeness as a goal for themselves or for their relationships. The fragmentation through which Cudjoe objectifies women becomes increasingly ironic considering that he attempts to find Simba and to "derail the tale" in order "to be whole again."

In his last conversation with Rachel, who is showing Cudjoe a painting she had painted for Sam before his death (possibly a sign of the creative and communicative depth of their relationship), Cudjoe can think only about Rachel's body. The way they end the encounter is revealing:

> I'll come to see you again. (He won't.) Let's keep in touch. (They are already out of touch.) Your painting is beautiful. (So it is and it changes nothing . . .) (71).

As with most of his interactions with women in the novel, language fails, indicating an absence of communication. And the episode of Cudjoe watching Cassandra, Sam and Rachel's daughter, bathe in the moonlight is especially significant for what she means to Sam and what Sam means to Cudjoe. Sam is described as Cudjoe's "twin, his cut buddy and drinking partner, voice of his conscience, stage manager of his art. . . . Didn't Sam teach him how to be anything?" (64). Sam is white, a successful

editor known for his power with language, the type of power Cudjoe
wishes to achieve. To Sam "Cassy was special. . . . Cassy was another
chance. . . . [at] a better Sam, reborn penitent, wiser for having sinned
grievously. Capable of unconditional love"(65). As with Cudjoe's having
to find Simba "to be whole again," Sam has his daughter who becomes
his "last goddamned chance" at being reborn. Cudjoe knows that her redemptive significance to Sam made Sam determined not to (figuratively
and literally) "fuck over this woman," but Cudjoe tells himself that "If
Sam had known how little time they could look forward to, together,
alive, wouldn't Sam have been there, beside him, greedily taking it all
in? His heart in his throat like Cudjoe's. His old pecker nudging his
shorts like Cudjoe's" (65). Reminiscent of Trueblood in Ralph Ellison's
Invisible Man, Cudjoe here reveals an openness to incest. In Cudjoe's
case, he imagines the incestuous relationship occurring between Sam
and his daughter, but the values expressed are Cudjoe's. Like Trueblood,
he reveals an important inadequacy in his identity as a man and a failure
in his own role as a father. While Cudjoe expresses a desire to "derail de
tale," and to bring about change, his openness to incest projects an accep-
tance of a closed system of nongrowth. Again, it presents Cudjoe's actions to be contradictory to change as he seems determined to affirm and
reproduce troubling negative stereotypes of black manhood.

In his own fatherly role, Cudjoe's inability to communicate effectively is also present. Wideman introduces Cudjoe's relationship to his
son in a scene depicting a phone call Cudjoe receives from prison. The
problems they have communicating, even through standard greetings,
suggests how Cudjoe's failure as a father is connected to his failure to
use language:

> I don't know what words mean when he says them. I don't know if he
> knows what they mean or knows why he says them. So we can't move
> beyond the ritual of greeting. To ask how he is opens a door into the
> chaos of our lives. Perhaps he is unable to tell me how he is. Perhaps I
> wouldn't understand how to take what he'd say, even if he tried to tell
> me. Words between us have become useless. Decorative. They can't
> furnish the empty rooms of our conversation. (99)

The above reflection reveals the fundamental inability Cudjoe and his
son have using language, and as a result, their inability to free Cudjoe
and his son from their being caged, both literally and figuratively. Later
in the narrative, Wideman juxtaposes two scenes in which Cudjoe's in-

ability to write his son's story is juxtaposed to his son's sitting in "limbo," gradually deteriorating while the legal system refuses to decide about removing his son's case from adult to juvenile court. Both characters "feel [their] narrative faculty weakening"; both are "going nowhere fast and also excruciatingly slowly" (115).

In his 1994 "meditation on fathers and sons," *Fatheralong*, Wideman addresses what he sees to be an inability of black fathers and sons to connect or to share a common language which will allow them to rewrite "a narrative of self":

> The stories must be told. Ideas of manhood, true and transforming, grow out of private, personal exchanges between fathers and sons. Yet for generations of black men in America this privacy, this privilege has been systematically breached in a most shameful and public way. . . . Generation after generation of black men, deprived of the voices of their fathers, are for all intents and purposes born semi-orphans. . . . Fathers in exile, in hiding, on the run, anonymous, undetermined, dead. The lost fathers cannot claim their own manhood. Speak first to themselves, then unambiguously to their sons. Arrayed against the possibility of conversation between fathers and sons is this country they inhabit, everywhere proclaiming the inadequacy of black fathers, their lack of manhood in almost every sense the term's understood here in America. (64-65)

Wideman makes clear in this passage, as he does in *Philadelphia Fire*, that to gain one's manhood is an issue of language. To be defined as a man, one must be included in the right conversations and must have a strong sense of identity fostered by an open line of communication with one's father. More important, one must have the right stories told about and to him. Being situated within language in this way, one is declared legitimately a man by the dominant discourse of society. And Cudjoe's failure to understand himself as "whole" stems largely from his systematic "inadiquacy" to use language effectively. He finds that his identity as "a parent who's lost a child" is one for which language has no word or place: "But what is the word for a parent who's lost a child? I have no word, no place to begin" (119). As for his son, language fails there as well: "You say nothing. Because the emptiness has no name, no place" (119). Cudjoe is unable to relate to his son because they share "an absence," a lack of language. Like the "void" of language which defines David in Baldwin's *Giovanni's Room*, Cudjoe's sense of his "manhood" is not whole because it is "forming around an absence we've been in the habit of calling one thing, but now it's another without a name, but I must speak to it, of it, exist with the pain of its presence and absence speaking to me a hundred times a day, every day" (120). As Cudjoe reflects upon his son's (and his own) attempt to construct an identity for himself from his caged position, he wonders if his son will not only become "locked in but also grateful for the cage of inactivity":

> To take stock, to make sense, to attempt to control or write a narrative of self—how hopeless any of these tasks must seem when the *self* attempting this harrowing business is no more reliable than a shadow, a chimera coming and going with a will or will-lessness of its own. . . . Is he doomed to fail? Doomed to come apart no matter how hard he struggles at constructing an identity, an ego, a life, an intimacy with who and what he is? Is madness the inevitable result? (110)

Both Cudjoe and his son lack power over language; they have nothing with which to write—or rewrite—identity. They have no self because "self-hood," as Wideman presents it in *Fatheralong*, originates in the narrative passed from father to son. Both father and narrative are absent, hence no origin.

Through the many failures of the black community and of the black government of Philadelphia to "derail the tale," Wideman suggests that "Words between [them] have become useless." Upon flying from Mykonos to Philadelphia, Cudjoe imagines setting "the city of brotherly love" in a crystal ball snow scene so that it won't be affected by the problems of history. One gets a sense that Cudjoe's reflection about the crystal ball applies to the "prison-house of language" which seems to be isolating members of the community from one another: "Nothing outside the sealed ball touches what's inside. Hermetic. Unreachable. Locked in and the key thrown away"(5-6). Instead of confronting the problems of history, which involves sharing a common language, the characters of *Philadelphia Fire* are more interested in sealing themselves off, each in their own protective shells. When Cudjoe returns to play basketball with other men of the community, the one scene Wideman includes in which black men seem to be bonding, sharing the common language of the sport, the ideology is not one of teamwork for the sake of common gain. Instead, Cudjoe points out that the game promotes a less unifying ideology: "The game's one on one on one. Every man for himself. You keep the pill as long as you can score" (34). And when Cudjoe makes an attempt to improve conditions for Blacks by talking to people and asking questions, the response he gets from Margaret Jones is to "Butt out"; she concludes that the people who started the fire thought they were helping and that the time for talking about the issue is long past. She desires such answers herself, but the idea of communicating positively with others to get them seems alien. Even the Philadelphia fire itself, as it is depicted in the novel, was a result of a lack of communication between King, the leader of the radical group MOVE, and the city's black mayor (not named in the novel, but in actuality Wilson Goode), who mutually find each other's attempts to improve black life in Philadelphia to be an embarrassment to Blacks.

Timbo, Cudjoe's friend and informant from inside the mayor's administration, tells Cudjoe that the new black mayor started out by advocating an ideology of working with others to bring about substantial change to improve conditions for all black people of the city, but soon that dream was lost, replaced with more "realistic" goals:

> He's realist about power and politics and deals and compromise and doing his jig inside the system. He ain't about change. He's about hanging on long enough so some who ain't never tasted the pie can have a bite before the whole shebang turns rotten. A simple, devious, practical man. (80-81)

Similar to the players in Cudjoe's basketball game, the black (and white) community take measures to improve conditions by promoting an ideology of "one on one on one."

The collective identity of Blacks in Philadelphia drifts into a madness of its own because it can't overcome a "will-lessness" of all the people individually acting on their own. Wideman's comments in his 1984 memoir, *Brothers and Keepers*, about his imprisoned brother Robbie, is particularly relevant here. Wideman writes that communication for Robbie "wouldn't make any difference," that the key to survival in such an imprisoned state is "learning to isolate himself": "If he doesn't insulate himself against those things he can't change, if he can't discipline himself to ignore and forget, to narrow the range of his concerns to what he can immediately, practically effect, he'll go crazy"(193). The collective "manhood" of the black community seems "doomed to fail" because as a body it is not whole. The members of the community, like Cudjoe's son and Wideman's brother, cannot "control or [re]write a narrative of self" because the business of survival compels them toward iso-

lation from and competition with each other and prevents them from
sharing a language to unify them. In one of the many short fragmented
passages which break up the novel, Wideman sums up the absolute isolation this narrational incapacity has brought about:

> Sometimes I've thought of myself, of you, of ourselves, as walled cities,
> each of us a fortress, a citadel, pinpoints of something that is the inverse
> of light, all of us in our profusion spread like maps of stars, each of us
> fixed in our place on a canvas immense beyond knowing, except that we
> know the immensity must be there to frame our loneliness, to separate
> us as far as we are separate each from each in the darkness. (120)

In what could possibly be an "inversion" of, or a play on, George Bush's
"thousand points of light," a systematic network of charities he envi-
sioned all working individually to bring about unity and better conditions
for all, Wideman's "pinpoints" are "something that is the inverse of
light," not a network at all because they don't share a common language.
These pinpoints work toward isolation and loneliness, against unification.

Cudjoe's attempt at being the fabulator by "rewriting" and producing his own version of *The Tempest* is perhaps his boldest move toward
unifying people with a common language. Producing a new set of roles
in which all of his actors are acting from the same script is itself a move
toward unification. Cudjoe's actors are children. They represent his desire to have a lasting impact with his "rewriting," and children also provide his play and Wideman's novel with a greater power to use language.
A child, Simba, is the driving force of the novel because of his imagined
capacity as a "tabula rasa," the blank slate on which to begin such
"rewriting." In the production of *The Tempest*, the children are noted as
important because of their capacity to use language as a unifying agent:

> You depend on children's capacity for make-believe. . . . little kids will
> whoop and holler, shriek with delight. Their enthusiasm will ignite the
> rest of the audience. We'll all be seized. Players. Play. Audience.
> Bound together by the screaming children. (149)

In a similar reflection about children from *Brothers and Keepers*, the significance of Cudjoe's fascination with child players and with Simba
becomes clearer:

> Kids use words that release hidden meanings, reveal history buried in sounds. They haven't forgotten that words can be more than signs, that words can be magic, the power to be things, to point to themselves and materialize. With their back-formations, archaisms, their tendency to play the music in words . . . children peel the skin from language. Words become incantory. Open Sesame. Abracadabra. Perhaps a child will remember the word that will bring the walls tumbling down. (34-5)

Of course, Cudjoe's choice of *The Tempest*, a play largely about language and magic, gains relevance in light of these reflections. And Simba's relevance as a magical transforming presence is highlighted here as well. Timbo remarks that Simba survived "everything in [the city's] arsenal" to destroy him because he is "Superkid, dig. . . . a symbol of kid power. He's a hero, magic. . . . Went through hell to show the others they can do it. Do anything" (91).

Cudjoe's desire to create a new discourse of growth by teaching the children of his play, by writing about Simba, and by finding some language to help his son write "a narrative of self" presents the positive side of Cudjoe's divided self, a side that is interested in unifying bodies—of communities and of language—instead of fragmenting them. But both sides of his divided self continue doing battle throughout the novel, and Wideman leaves much to suggest that "will-lessness" will not be easily beaten. In Cudjoe's production of *The Tempest*, "will-lessness" seems to become naturalized as, ironically, the production of the play is cancelled due to rain, a tempest. Such natural frustrations seem to confirm the frustration he already feels as a fabulator:

> You can't just rewrite the Tempest any old way you please. . . . Play got to end as it always does. Prospero still the boss. Master of ceremonies. Spinning the wheel of fortune. Having the last laugh. Standing there thinking he's cute telling everybody what to do next. And people can't wait to clap their hands and say thanks. (144)

The capacity of Cudjoe's actors to make believe and unify people is never tapped, and, at least by the novel's end, Cudjoe never does find Simba to write a new mythology. Ultimately, the ability of Cudjoe to produce any change at all is left in question. Cudjoe's final message to his son seems to encompass all that Cudjoe fails to achieve as a fabulator:

> Can you learn to hope in what seems a hopeless situation? . . . I don't feel I can tell you anything."(150)

Language fails Cudjoe as he is left feeling powerless to communicate any compelling reason for his son to hope outside of, "We do have a chance to unfold our days one by one and piece together a story that shapes us. It's the only life anyone ever has. Hold on"(151). Set against the background of Cudjoe's failure to write a new story that can reshape his own life, any hope offered in such advice largely falls flat.

In the final scene of the novel, one year after the fire, Cudjoe visits a memorial ceremony for the fire victims in Philadelphia's Independence Square. Wideman packs the scene with much evidence to suggest that even at this ceremony, designed to confront history and to unify people with a common cause, the frustrations preventing the creation of a new unifying and redemptive discourse are still present. Cudjoe is surprised by how poorly attended the memorial ceremony is. It seems there is a "will-lessness" of the people to remember and to use that memory as a foundation for reconstructing a narrative of hope. And Wideman constructs this final scene with many references to the powerlessness of language. Cudjoe notes that the words used to recite the victims' names are "shell, husk, earthbound"; in effect they are empty and lifeless. He also note that the balloons which are released in honor of the victims are, as a sign, empty: he doesn't know what they mean to him, and they provide "no sign the lost souls have been welcomed or refused"(198). Cudjoe's lack of power to use language seems sealed as he can't memorize the victims' names: "Not time to learn them before they became something else, whisked away, elsewhere, where they would always be, waiting gone"(198). He adds that the names of the victims used to bind elements, "Fire . . . Water. Earth. Air," and "breathed life into their combinations" (198), but now the names are like the balloons, fleeting, and insubstantial. The children of this scene are the dead victims, so their potential to ignite the audience or bring walls tumbling down seems present—or absent—only in the insubstantiality of their names. And the poor attendance at this memorial suggests that few, if any, will attend the next one. The program ends because, fittingly, the "people on stage and in the audience sense there's nothing more to say"(198).

In the last paragraph of the novel, Wideman seems to change gears in that Cudjoe has "words come to him, cool him, stop him in his tracks"(199). The final suggestion is that, as Cudjoe advises his son earlier, "The picture changes, if only because you've lived through one more day of hell"(151). All evidence to the contrary, hope, however uncertain and muted, still exists. The words calling out to Cudjoe, "Never again, never again" have been known by him all his life; they are words that occupy a place in his "divided self" which may someday lead to a substantial rewriting of his self. Cudjoe also notes that he sometimes believes the children of his play are still reciting their lines. And most significantly, the novel ends with Simba still "out there," with his potential to be transgressive and redemptive intact.

In a 1988 interview with James Coleman, Wideman states that

> . . . both plots and themes of the fictions I write, and the fictions themselves, are an attempt to subvert one notion of reality with others, to show that there is not simply one way of seeing things but many ways of seeing things. And as a people and as individuals if we don't jump into the breach, if we don't fight the battle of defining reality on our own terms, then somebody else will always come along and do it for us.(151-2)

Perhaps the greatest hope that the fiction, *Philadelphia Fire*, has to offer lies in its insistence that black men have the potential, however much unrealized, to "rewrite" their lives. Wideman's own radically liberating use of narrative technique is evidence that, Cudjoe's failure to do so notwithstanding, tales can be told in more than one way. But if Wideman is successful in "defining reality on his own terms," he also suggests that success may be undercut by the lack of substance found in technique on its own. The novel does provide a model of a man who has control over discourse, Cudjoe's friend, Sam; but nothing about the outcome of his life suggests that he has found the redemption through language that Cudjoe—and Wideman—seek. Although Sam is not black, he is described by Cudjoe as "a great man. A successful writer, editor." In this description, Sam's greatness as a man seems connected to his ability to write and to "rewrite." His philosophy about great writing and advice to Cudjoe is that technique is central to truly transgressive writing: "Technique, technique, my bucko, is truth"(64). Since *Philadelphia Fire* is so boldly experimental in various forms of technique, one would assume Wideman is taking his own character's advice. But Wideman leaves no suggestion that technique by itself is a redemptive force for Sam. Like Cudjoe, Sam's "last goddamned chance" at redemption is a child, and she dies in her own tragic fire before her redemptive potential can be realized. Her death is the end of the substance of his life; it causes the slow deterioration that ultimately kills him. And Sam fails to leave Cudjoe, his best student, with any power to use language to "derail de tale" or to be an effective teacher with his own students. Sam's repetition of the words, "Teach me" upon his own death suggests that even this "great man,

writer, and editor" dies with much to learn about the redemptive power
of language.

Whereas Sam's own failure to use language to "rewrite" his own
life suggests a major contradiction in Wideman's novel—the failure of
technique in a novel that obviously flaunts technique, I suggest that the
contradiction itself shows the depth to which Wideman approaches post-
modernism. The political nature of *Philadelphia Fire* makes it clear that
Wideman's own approach toward change involves a commitment beyond
technique. Technique is certainly a tool toward discursive change, but for
that change to have any substance, "will-lessness," along with debilitating social and political discourses must be overcome. Technique must be
anchored by a commitment to some sense of meaning in order to survive
the "tempestuous" forces denying black men like Cudjoe a sense of
wholeness.

In *Philadelphia Fire*, Wideman suggests that black men—and black
people of urban America in general—remain essentially disenfranchised
largely because they are driven to remain preoccupied with the "one on
one on one" business of survival. Such an ideology fosters ignoring and
forgetting, more than it does controlling language or rewriting narratives.
Wideman's own fiction writing, like his memoir writing, has the tremen-
dous power it does because of much more than masterful technique.
Wideman posits himself as a controller of language, one who literally
writes his own story; and, more importantly, he overcomes will-lessness,
making a commitment to give his fictions lasting substance. With such a
commitment he has a chance to "fight the battle to define reality" and
win.

CHAPTER 4

Ernest Gaines:
A Lesson About Manhood
Appropriating "The Word"
in *A Lesson Before Dying*

> *The word in language is half someone else's.*
> *It becomes "one's own" only when the speaker*
> *populates it with his own intention, his own*
> *accent, when he appropriates the word, adapt-*
> *ing it to his own semantic and expressive inten-*
> *tion. Prior to the moment of appropriation, the*
> *word does not exist in a neutral and impersonal*
> *language . . . , but rather it exists in other*
> *people's mouths, in other people's contexts,*
> *serving other people's intentions: it is from*
> *there that one must take the word and make it*
> *one's own.*
> —MIKHAIL BAKHTIN, "DISCOURSE IN THE NOVEL"

> *If we must die, let it not be like hogs*
> *Hunted and penned in an inglorious spot . . .*
> *If we must die, O let us nobly die,*
> *So that our precious blood may not be shed*
> *In vain . . .*
> —CLAUDE MCKAY, "IF WE MUST DIE"

From Ernest Gaines' earliest published works of the late fifties and the sixties to his most recent novel, *A Lesson Before Dying*, Gaines consistently writes about black men who face the problems of being denied the dignity and self-worth found in the status of "manhood." In *A Lesson Before Dying*, Gaines again picks up this theme as the narrator of the story, Grant Wiggins, a black college-educated school teacher, takes on the responsibility of convincing Jefferson, a non-educated black laborer who has been sentenced to death for a murder he didn't commit, that Jefferson is indeed a "man," and not a "hog" as his white attorney declared as part of his defense strategy:

Do you see a modicum of intelligence? Do you see anyone here could
plan a murder. . . . a cornered animal to strike quickly out of fear, but to
plan? . . . I would as soon put a hog in the electric chair as this. (7-8)

While much of Gaines' work addresses the issue of establishing
manhood, *A Lesson Before Dying* is distinct in that it focuses on this
issue in a most direct way: the problem Grant and Jefferson are faced
with is a problem of redefining Jefferson, from the identity given to him
by the dominant white culture, hog, to a new identity, man.

Within the scope of this problem, *A Lesson Before Dying* explores
the roles of social institutions such as education, law, and especially religion as they all have a part in producing human dignity and self-worth. It
is in the mythologies and ideologies that these social institutions produce
that the foundations for definition and identity are created. Jefferson does
feel that he has experienced a change in identity by the novel's end, and
that change is made possible through his and the black community's appropriation of social institutions and of myths and ideologies themselves. Similar to Baldwin, Walker, and Wideman, Gaines recognizes
that for a change in personal and social identity to have any lasting "substance," language itself, in this case the complete make-up of discursive
formations surrounding Jefferson, must also change. More specifically,
Jefferson's becoming a man at the novel's end is an act based on the reinscription of (among other things) a most essential foundation for discourse, the bible. In this case, Jefferson is understood as a man because
his life first takes on Christ-like significance.

In defining discourse and its social power, Michel Foucault writes
that the discursive power of a doctor, the power to present and sanction
truth, is socially determined through a network of systematic authorization involving medical, judiciary, educational, and even religious representation:

. . . discourse is not the majestically unfolding manifestation of a thinking, knowing, speaking subject, but, on the contrary, a totality . . . (50)

Of course, it is this totality of discursive power that overwhelms
other key characters of this study such as Wright's Bigger Thomas, Baldwin's David, Walker's Brownfield and Wideman's Cudjoe. It is in this respect that I see the task before Jefferson and Grant taking on such great
significance. Jefferson is a "hog" for the same reason Bigger and Brownfield take on animalistic identities, because the socially dominant system

of inscription, white-supremacist patriarchy, deems him so. In effect, for any act of redefinition on Jefferson or Grant's part to have any lasting impact, the totality of systematic networks of authorization must be breached.

It is important to remember that although Jefferson's symbolic role in the novel is central, this is Grant's story. Grant is the novel's narrative voice, and he is the person given the primary responsibility of transforming the status of Jefferson from hog to "man." Obviously, Grant's own situation is somewhat similar to Jefferson's in that both he and Jefferson undergo a profound change in their own self-perceptions. Grant doesn't want the responsibility for initiating this transformation mostly because he feels any effort made toward this end would be futile. Grant makes it clear that even he, a black man who has become college educated, cannot express himself in the way he wishes in his community. He finds his own freedom extremely limited, if it is indeed existent at all, and he sees the future of his students to be lacking in any promise of advancement. He realizes, for instance, that the work his students perform at the schoolhouse, chopping wood and other menial chores, is the same work they will likely have in the future:

> And I thought to myself, What am I doing? Am I reaching them at all? They are doing exactly what the old men did earlier. They are fifty years younger, maybe more, but doing the same thing those old men did who never attended school a day in their lives. Is it just a vicious circle? Am I doing anything? (62)

Grant feels that his role as an educator bears no promise of producing change either, for he finds that he must work to promote the dominant white-supremacist ideology—or not work at all. Grant is doing the same work and teaching the same ideas that his own teacher, Matthew Antoine, had taught a generation earlier. And Grant has come to share Mr. Antoine's pessimistic conclusions as well: " 'It doesn't matter anymore,' he said. 'Just do the best you can. But it won't matter' " (66).

Grant realizes that the powerlessness of Jefferson is, in fact, not so different from the powerlessness he himself feels. Whereas Jefferson is imprisoned in a literally confining structure of white law, Grant is also imprisoned within the structures of white discourse. The most obvious example of such discursive confinement is that of the educational system. The schoolhouse itself is a detention camp of sorts in which Grant is allowed to teach only the ideology that will keep himself and his black community powerless. And Dr. Joseph, the school superintendent, is, in effect, the warden whose role is to make sure Grant and the students stay powerless. Grant even sees some telling significance in the way Dr. Joseph inspects the school children:

> And besides looking at hands, now he began inspecting teeth. Open wide, say 'Ahhh'—and he would have the poor children spreading out their lips as far as they could while he peered into their mouths. At the university I had read about slave masters who had done the same when buying new slaves. . . . (56)

Gaines emphasizes the complete imprisoning function of white discourse through the many "structures" he selects for the voice(s) of white patriarchy. Mr. Pichot, a powerful white land owner whom Grant's aunt goes to for help, and his group of the town's patriarchal elite often take refuge in Pichot's library, a structure designed to surround one with white-supremacist ideology as it is presented in his books; the sheriff is often behind his desk at the prison; the group of white men who declare Jefferson a murderer are found within the confines of the courtroom. Even Dr. Joseph is secure in his "confining structure"—the school house. The connection to be made is clear: these white men are so powerful not simply because they are positioned in such architectural structures; instead, their power is supported by the discursive structures that they are all, in return, to uphold and enforce. These discursive structures—of ideology, law, and ultimately language itself—are, literally and figuratively, structures designed to preserve white forms of power. These structures are the manifestations of power Foucault refers to when he speaks of discursive totality. For black members of this southern community, such "structures" of white patriarchy are there to disempower, to convict, to imprison, to enslave.

Grant's aunt Tante Lou, Jefferson's godmother Miss Emma, and Reverend Ambrose learn to deal with such oppression through their faith in the institution of religion. Grant, however, sees religion as doing little to produce change. The prayers his students recite are the same ones he recited as a student, and the Christmas play his students perform hasn't changed, nor has it proven to effect change. Grant has as little "faith" in institutional religious practice as he does in his own ability to produce change within the educational system.

In order to subvert a discursive formation that defines Jefferson as a hog, Grant comes to learn that simply recognizing the problems that cause such injustice is not enough; nor is it enough to "put one's faith" in institutionalized religion which seems to promote passivity and patience more than any active approach to change. The change that is needed is one in which the foundations for definition, for identity, are subverted. And although Grant isn't necessarily aware of the changes he is helping to bring about, Gaines presents the solution to changing identity as nothing short of a revolutionary discursive shift, built upon an entirely new rhetorical foundation for language itself.

In discussing the relationship between language and the cultural critic who presents himself as the agent of change, Terry Eagleton, in *Walter Benjamin: Or Towards a Revolutionary Criticism*, provides a significant "anatomy" of revolution which is certainly applicable to Gaines' novel:

> To say that [a text] is 'true' is not to state that it represents a real state of affairs. It is to claim that the text so fictionalizes the 'real' as to intend a set of effects conducive to certain practices that are deemed, in light of a particular set of falsifiable hypotheses about the nature of society, to be desirable. . . . The practice of the [revolutionary] cultural worker, in brief, is projective, polemical, and appropriative. (113)

In theorizing "toward a revolutionary criticism," Eagleton writes that even a marxist critic like himself must—to a certain extent—become a Platonist, advocating an absolutist philosophy to which, by nature, Marxists stand in opposition. In other words, since all truth is based on relational discursive formations (and is therefore fictional), the agent of change should move beyond the inevitable fictionality of his or her position and be more interested in doing all that he or she can to promote his or her desired ends. If that means appropriating the language of the opposition, then so be it.

The theory I aim to pose in this study is that the lesson Gaines puts forth in *A Lesson Before Dying* is one similar to Eagleton's revolutionary theory: that producing change is ultimately a rhetorical act. If one's goal is to change identity, one must subvert the dominant discursive formations themselves. Only with such a foundational change can hogs become men.

In subverting the white power structure Grant does understand part of what he and Jefferson have to do:

> "Do you know what myth is, Jefferson?" I asked him. "A myth is an old lie that people believe in. White people believe that they're better

than anyone else on earth—and that's a myth. The last thing they ever
want is to see a black man stand, and think, and to show that common
humanity that is in us all. It would destroy their myth." (192)

Grant understands in order to destroy the myth of white supremacy, it is
their job to show its falseness. What Grant doesn't understand is that in
destroying one myth he is being, in Eagleton's words, "projective,
polemical and appropriative" in that he must replace one myth with another. Grant sees that white power is based on lies; he comes to learn
from Reverend Ambrose that to produce a feeling of power for the black
community, he must lie as well:

> "Yes, you know. You know, all right. That's why you look down on me,
> because you know I lie. At wakes, at funerals, at weddings—yes, I lie. I
> lie at wakes and funerals to relieve pain. 'Cause reading, writing, and
> 'rithmatic is not enough. You think that's all they sent you to school
> for? They sent you to school to relieve pain, to relieve hurt—and if you
> have to lie to do it, then you lie. You lie and you lie and you lie." (218)

As I suggested earlier, the lies that keep the black community so oppressed and keep Jefferson from gaining his "manhood" are ingrained
deeply in the social institutions which control discourse. If one can gain
control of these institutions, one can control the mythology that produces
identity. The "lying" that Grant produces takes shape in the way that he,
Tante Lou, Miss Emma, and the entire black community work together
to do more than simply destroy the white-supremacist mythology; they
effectively replace that mythology with one of their own.

It is the first priority for Jefferson's godmother—as initiator of this
new mythology and, ultimately, the reinscription of Jefferson—to penetrate the cage of white-supremacist discourse which surrounds him. And
for that reason, her and Tante Lou's insistence on entering Jefferson's
prison cell is significant; their success represents the first ray of hope that
the "prison-house of language" can be breached.

The many images Gaines provides of Jefferson's family, Reverend
Ambrose, and other members of the community entering the prison to be
with Jefferson are also significant, for they show how the forces which
create ideology and mythology, such as communal affirmation, education, and religion, are allowed to penetrate white discourse. Just as the legitimacy of Pichot's patriarchal power is confirmed by his various forms
of social affirmation—especially in the way he usually surrounds him-

self with the support of other patriarchs, so it is that Jefferson will ultimately reach some feeling of self-worth.

Yet, this step is only the beginning. The abundance of communal affirmation given to Jefferson gives him symbolic and even iconographic value. The image of his kneeling to gain forgiveness is an important one for Reverend Ambrose, and the image of his standing with pride upon facing his death is the image his aunt and the community want confirmed in the end. With this in mind, the new mythology being created is one in which Jefferson becomes a Christ-figure in that his divinity, his centrality as a transcendental meta-signifier, is the power that allows for his "manhood" to become a reality. Like Christ he is both God and man. What Grant comes to learn by the end of this experience is that change isn't built upon a simple eradication of the old God. Instead, he and the black community have to produce a new God, one who can confirm the community's human dignity. He learns that in order to redefine a man, one must first redefine God.

Gaines overtly presents the establishment of those who "play God" as representing discursive power. Similar to the "God-like" patriarchs of Walker's *The Third Life of Grange Copeland*, white patriarchy are the God figures of this novel; they control discursive power to confirm or deny humanity. The point Gaines makes of having Jefferson defined in animalistic terms by white patriarchy, a definition he comes to believe himself, mirrors Walker's treatment of Brownfield's being entrapped in white discourse. After he realizes that they have "come up with the time and the date to take the life of another man," Grant asks "Who made them God?" And, of course, Grant asks a similar question about himself when he begins to understand the significance of the task being asked of him:

> The jury, twelve white men good and true, still sentenced him to death.
> Now his godmother wants me to visit him and make him know—prove
> to these white men—that he's not a hog, that he's a man. Who am I?
> God? (31)

In another point thematically similar to Walker's, this passage makes clear the power that the God-figure has in creating identity. So much so that when Vivian is asked by Tante Lou about the future of her religious affiliation, the phrasing is especially poignant: "You'll leave your church and just become—nothing?" (114). Similarly, in the Christmas play put on by Grant's students, the scene they recreate emphasizes the power of the God-figure to take the "nothings" of the world and give them self-worth:

> Shepherd Two: But we ain't nothing but poor little old shepherds.
> Wise Man One: The lowest is the highest in His eyes. (149)

The transformation of Jefferson into a God-figure is also foreshadowed by Grant's reflection on the God-like significance of Joe Louis to the black community:

> I could still remember how depressed everyone was after Joe had lost the first fight to Schmeling. For weeks it was like that. To be caught laughing for any reason was a sin. This was a period of mourning. What else in the world was there to be proud of, if Joe had lost? Even the preacher got into it. "Let us wait. Let us wait, children. David will meet Goliath again." (88)

And after Louis' win in the rematch, Grant remembers the explosion of pride in his community: "For days after the fight, for weeks, we held our heads higher than any people on earth had done for any reason"(89). The symbolic power of this black man resisting and defeating the white heavy-weight champion makes him God-like in that he is a positive creator of identity for his black following. The preacher's sermonizing about Louis proves his mythological importance. It is in this victory of biblical proportions that Louis' followers gain their "manhood."

In Jefferson's resistance to the white patriarchal labeling of him as a hog, Ernest Gaines shows that such resistance makes Jefferson similar in God-like stature to Louis. In fact, Gaines overtly establishes the Christ-like significance of Jefferson. Besides the obvious connection of this innocent man being put to death for less than just cause, Jefferson's death is timed by the town's officials so as not to conflict with a religious holiday, as Christ's death was timed by Roman and Jewish authorities so as not to coincide with the Jewish Sabbath. The actual span of Jefferson's life in prison is from the Christmas season to the Easter season. And the moment of his death occurs appropriately " . . . on Friday. Same time as He died, between twelve and three" (158). His status as a Christ-figure is further established in his wish to die as "He" did, without "a mumbling word," and the connection is perhaps most explicit in that he realizes that what Grant is asking is that he "take the cross" of others:

'Me, Mr. Wiggins. Me. Me to take the cross. Your cross, nannan's cross,
my own cross. Me, Mr. Wiggins. This old stumbling nigger. Y'all axe a
lot, Mr. Wiggins.' (224)

Jefferson's Christ-like significance establishes an allegorical dimen-
sion to *A Lesson Before Dying* which reinforces the role of myth in the
re-creation of Jefferson. With Jefferson as the Christ, Miss Emma, Jefferson's *god*mother takes on the role usually reserved for God the father:
she is the initiator of the discursive movement; from her ultimately
springs a new identity for Jefferson and his "followers." In this sense she
has the creative potential associated with God. Her role as god*mother* is
also significant in that it establishes the new mythology being created as
at least partially matriarchal. This may be Gaines' way of expressing the
fullness of this discursive shift away from both whiteness and patriarchy,
and it may also be a statement by Gaines about an absence of father figures in such impoverished black communities of the deep south. But it is
important to note that although Gaines presents Miss Emma as giving up
her power to Grant and Reverand Ambrose after she initiates the discursive shift, her principal role as a provider of physical nourishment in the
form of the food she makes is another symbol of her continued leader-
ship and of Jefferson's Christ-like significance. The physical nourishment she provides mirrors the *meta*physical nourishment he obtains from
the other "god-figures," mainly Grant and Reverend Ambrose. And, of
course, the combination of the physical and the metaphysical is, according to Christian theology, a major part of the significance of Christ.

The allegorical resonance of Jefferson as Christ-figure is again compounded by Gaines' inclusion of Jefferson's journal. In it Jefferson relates all of the simple expressions of love he encounters in the final days
before his death. He includes passages about many firsts: the first time he
told somebody (Grant) "i like you," the first time members of the community, including the handicapped Bok, show him expressions of love,
and the first time he experiences such affection for and from his godmother:

> ... an i tol her i love her an i tol her i was strong an she jus look ole
> and tied an pull me to her an kis me an it was the firs she never done
> that it felt good an i let her long is she want ... (231)

Perhaps the most important first of the journal lies in his confirmation
that Grant's efforts have paid off:

. . . i cry cause you been so good to me mr wigin an nobody ain't never
been that good to make me think im somebody . . . (232)

Jefferson shows with abundance the power to be gained in the spirit
of mutual giving. Jefferson and the members of his community all gain
in their actualizations of self-worth as they give to each other. Perhaps a
significant distinction to be acknowledged here is that Jefferson as a rein-
scribed God is not the vengeful God of law represented in the Old Testament. The patriarchs of the white community take on this role. Instead,
Jefferson becomes the giving God of faith and love of the New Testament. His power resides in his ability to make people believe that "to
give is to receive." Obviously the form of Jefferson's discourse, as written, takes on religious significance as well. In line with his significance
as a Christ-figure, he leaves behind "the word," a biblical text which can
be read as a guide to "love[ing] one another." In this regard Jefferson provides a literally "new testament" of great symbolic weight.

And along with the allegorical impact Jefferson's writing has as a
biblical text, one must not overlook the symbolic and revolutionary impact to be found simply in the act of Jefferson's writing. In "Writing
'Race' and the Difference it Makes," Henry Louis Gates puts this idea in
perspective as he discusses the symbolic importance of writing in western culture in the eighteenth century:

> Writing, especially after the printing press became so widespread, was
> taken to be the *visible* sign of reason. Blacks were "reasonable" and
> hence "men," if—and only if—they demonstrated mastery over "the
> arts and sciences," the eighteenth century's formula for writing. (8)

Although the plot of Gaines' novel is, of course, set well after the
eighteenth century, a similar argument is used by Jefferson's attorney in
declaring Jefferson's lack of manhood; he notes Jefferson's illiteracy as
proof of this lack:

> 'Oh sure, he has reached the age of twenty-one, when we, civilized
> men, consider the male species has reached manhood, but would you
> call this—this—this a man? No, not I. . . . Mention the names of Keats,
> Byron, Scott, and see whether his eyes will show one moment of
> recognition. Ask him to describe a rose, to quote from one passage of
> the Constitution or the Bill of Rights.'(8)

Set against this white patriarchal prescription for manhood, Jefferson's writing must be recognized as a radical act in itself. Of course,

Grant's college education is seen as a threat to Pichot and his fellow patriarchs. But Jefferson's writing isn't simply a cry for legitimacy in white culture. Perhaps his writing "across the lines instead of above them," as well as his already noted concentration on the issue of mutual giving, is indication enough that Jefferson's discourse is "going in a different direction," truly a "new testament" of how legitimacy and manhood can be obtained and enacted.

Into this unfolding, biblically allegorical scheme that *A Lesson Before Dying* takes on, the significance of Paul, the guard who befriends Grant and Jefferson, seems to fit almost too neatly. Like his namesake of the New Testament, Paul is the converted soldier struck by a "bolt of lightning" to ultimately preach "the word" of the Christ:

> 'I heard the two jolts, but I wouldn't look up. I'll never forget the sound of the generator as long as I live on this earth.' . . . 'Allow me to be your friend Grant Wiggins. I don't ever want to forget this day. I don't ever want to forget him.' (254-5)

Paul's eagerness to read the journal after Grant is finished and to help Grant spread "the word" to his students that Jefferson was the "bravest man" at the execution extends the parallel with the biblical St. Paul. And perhaps the most significant connection to his biblical namesake rests in the importance St. Paul places on justification by faith above the law:

> Therefore, since we are justified by faith, we have peace with God through our Lord Jesus Christ. Through him we have obtained access to this grace in which we stand, and we rejoice in our hope of sharing the glory of God. More than that, we rejoice in our sufferings, knowing that suffering produces endurance, and endurance produces character, and character produces hope, and hope does not disappoint us. (Romans 5:1-5)

One can easily imagine Gaines' character giving a similar formula for hope to Grant's students.

Grant tells Paul in the final chapter of the novel that "You have to believe to be a good teacher" (254), and Paul then bears witness about the transformation Grant's teaching produced. In the creation of this new Christ, Grant and his community have created, and "share the glory" of, someone they can believe in. Grant's original hope of debunking faith arose from the problems he had with the form the Christ figure takes in the white dominant discourse—a white patriarch. Grant learns that his role as an agent of change is not simply to debunk the myth but to appropriate it—to reinscribe it, so it works toward his and his community's own ends. Ultimately, the teaching of St. Paul rings true for Grant. Throughout the novel he struggles to find something to believe in; in the end he finds it in Jefferson, *and* he finds it in himself. It is important to note that the meaning he is seeking, his own justification, is not obtained by realizing any "tangible" results: Jefferson still dies unjustly, and the black community is still fundamentally oppressed. Yet, Grant, Paul and the members of the black community have received "justification by faith."

Since "tangible" results have not been realized, one must ask about the "actual" limits of power gained by this discursive reinscription of Christian myth. Can Grant now be as subversive as he pleases in the classroom? Does Paul stand a chance as a white police officer preaching about black "manhood" in a white-supremacist, southern black town? The answers to these questions seem less than hopeful. One can hear the voice of Sheriff Guidry holding the novel's hopeful ending in check: " . . . the first sign of aggravation, I'm calling it off"(50). His voice, as representative of white patriarchal law, suggests that although Miss Emma and Grant have been able to penetrate white discourse, they have also been contained within it. Their interaction with Jefferson, always within the county jail, would seem to confirm this. However, the transformation of Paul confirms that some "substantial" change has been effected. Although Paul is acknowledged from the beginning as being "from good stock," he is also a representative of white patriarchal law. His change has its greatest value in its symbolic importance: it shows that white patriarchy has not contained this new discourse; instead, white patriarchy is now being changed, not just penetrated. While "practical," "substantial" change still seems remote, the symbolic power in the transformations of the black community and especially of Paul shows that the potential for such change is great.

And perhaps that potential is the most significant New Testament connection of all. Christ's presence in the New Testament signifies the *promise* of eternal life—not its fulfillment. Fulfillment will come in the future, and not for all, but for those who will have faith. As with Christ's, Jefferson's symbolic value has only begun in his death. The point here is that *A Lesson Before Dying*, like the New Testament, resists closure. It is the novel itself that confirms the promise of the "projective" power within the "appropriation of the word." The transformative power that Jefferson's word has on Grant and on Paul is projected to readers in

Grant's (gospel) narration. The novel itself becomes the promise renewed and extended.

Ultimately, the *Lesson Before Dying* that Ernest Gaines provides is a lesson about manhood. Like the other writers in this study, Gaines provides his own "rewriting" of black manhood, in this case with a story very similar to Wright's *Native Son*. While Bigger Thomas remains existentially entrapped in his "cage" of white discourse at the end of Wright's novel, Gaines provides some hope that the totality of white discourse can be overcome. He makes it clear that "being a man," especially for a black man in the white-supremacist south, has everything to do with appropriating discursive power, and the potential is there for that to happen. For Jefferson, as for the white patriarchs of his community, the power to define oneself and to define others is confirmed in the ideologies produced by the social structures of culture. With this in mind, Gaines shows how becoming a man is ultimately an act of mythic and, in this case, biblical proportions.

Establishing New Spaces

*We must continue inventing our story, sustain-
ing the double consciousness that is necessary
for any writing with the ambition of forging its
own place.*

—JOHN EDGAR WIDEMAN
"THE ARCHITECTONICS OF FICTION"

In discussing "the fate of the black story in a white world of white stories," John Edgar Wideman asserts that "if black writers want freedom,"
their stories "should somehow contain clues that align [them] with tradition and critique tradition, establish the new space [they] require"(45). I
see this "double-conscious" dynamic informing the works of Baldwin,
Walker, Wideman, and Gaines discussed in this study. Whereas this dissertation certainly recognizes the influence of one author on many, it is
focused more on the new space each writer creates in order to invent his
or her own story, spaces which in turn open more space for future stories
to be written and rewritten.

With the rise in feminism since the 1960s the writing(s) of black
women has flourished, making many new, highly visible, spaces for redefining black womanhood. The huge exposure of Alice Walker's *The
Color Purple* and the world recognition of the writing of Toni Morrison
with her recent Pulitzer and Nobel prizes are just two examples of the ex-
pansiveness of discursive space being forged by black women. Similarly,
the rise in "men's studies" of the late 1980s to the present is sparking a
new awareness—and reinforcing the not-so-new feminist awareness—
that the narratives of black men do not simply represent *the voice* of the
black community in America. As our awareness of race *and* gender concerns comes together, it becomes obvious that black men, as black men,
have their own stories to invent, their own discursive space(s) to establish.

Within two months of the completion of this dissertation, Ballantine
Books published *Brotherman: The Odyssey of Black Men in America—*

An Anthology, edited by Herb Boyd and Robert L. Allen. In this age of gender awareness, it is hard to believe that this anthology is actually the first published anthology specifically about black men. Considering this fact I feel that this study is, at least, timely. I know that this book is not the first of its kind to study literature specifically about concerns of black men. It is heartening to know, however, that in its own way, it is establishing its own discursive space—aligned with tradition and critiquing it as well.

Works Cited

Abbandonato, Linda. "Rewriting the Heroine's Story in *The Color Purple*." Eds. Henry Louis Gates and K.A. Appiah. *Alice Walker: Critical Perspectives Past and Present*. New York: Amistad, 1993. (pp. 296-308).

Adams, Stephen. "*Giovanni's Room*: The Homosexual as Hero." Ed. Harold Bloom. *Modern Critical Views: James Baldwin*. New York: Chelsea, 1986. (pp. 131-139).

Baker, Houston A., Jr. "On Knowing our Place." Eds. Henry Louis Gates, Jr. and K. A. Appiah. *Richard Wright: Critical Perspectives Past and Present* New York: Amistad Press, 1993.

————. *The Journey Back: Issues in Black Literature and Criticism*. Chicago: University of Chicago Press, 1980.

Bakhtin, Mikhail. *The Dialogic Imagination: Four Essays*. Ed. Michael Holquist. Texas: University of Texas Press, 1981.

Baldwin, James. *Giovanni's Room*. 1956 rpt. New York: Dell Publishing, 1988.

————. "Everybody's Protest Novel." *Notes of a Native Son*. 1955rpt. Boston: Beacon Press, 1984. (pp. 13-23).

————. "Alas Poor Richard." *Nobody Knows My Name: More Notes of a Native Son*. 1961 rpt. New York: Vintage Books, 1993. (pp. 181-189).

————. "Many Thousands Gone." *Notes of a Native Son*. 1955 rpt. Boston: Beacon Press, 1984. (pp. 24-45).

————. "The Black Boy Looks at the White Boy." *Nobody Knows My Name: More Notes of a Native Son*. 1961 rpt. New York: Vintage Books, 1993. (pp. 216-241).

Bigsby, C.W.E. "The Divided Mind of James Baldwin." ed. Fred L. Standley and Nancy V. Burt. *Critical Essays on James Baldwin*. Boston: G.K. Hall and Company, 1988. (pp. 94-110).

Boyd, Herb and Robert L. Allen (Eds.) *Brotherman: The Odyssey of Black Men in America—An Anthology.* New York: Ballantine Books, 1995.

Butler, Robert James. "Making a Way Out of No Way: The Open Journey in Alice Walker's *The Third Life of Grange Copeland.*" *Black American Literature Forum*, 22.1. (Spring 1988). 65-79.

Campbell, James. *Talking at the Gates: A Life of James Baldwin.* New York: Viking, 1991.

Clausen, Jan. "Native Fathers." *The Kenyon Review.* 14.2. (Spring 1992). 44-55.

Cleaver, Eldridge. *Soul on Ice.* 1968 rpt. New York: Dell Publishing, 1992.

Coleman, James. *Blackness and Modernism: The Literary Career of John Edgar Wideman.* Jackson: University Press of Mississippi, 1989.

DeGout, Yasmin Y. "Dividing the Mind: Contradictory Portraits of Homoerotic Love in *Giovanni's Room.*" *African American Review.* 28.3 (1992). 425-435.

Dubois, W.E.B. *The Souls of Black Folk.* New York: Bantam Books, 1989.

Eagleton, Terry. *Walter Benjamin: Or Toward a Revolutionary Criticism.* London: Verso, 1988.

Foucault, Michel. *The Archaeology of Knowledge.* rpt. 1969. trans. A.M. Sheridan Smith. New York: Pantheon Books, 1972.

France, Alan W. "Misogyny and Appropriation in *Native Son.*" *Modern Fiction Studies.* 34.3 (1988). 413-423.

Gaines, Ernest. *A Lesson Before Dying.* New York: Alfred A. Knopf, 1993.

Gates, Henry Louis. (Ed.) "Writing 'Race' and the Difference it Makes." *"Race," Writing, and Difference.* Chicago: University of Chicago Press, 1986. (pp. 1-20).

———. Introduction to *The Souls of Black Folk* by W.E.B. Dubois. New York: Bantam Books, 1989. (pp. vii-xxix).

———. Preface to *Richard Wright: Critical Perspectives Past and Present.* Eds. Henry Louis

Gates, Jr. and K. A. Appiah. New York: Amistad Press, 1993.

Hernton, Calvin. *The Sexual Mountain and Black Women Writers: Adventures in Sex, Literature, and Real Life.* New York: Doubleday, 1987.

Hogue, W. Lawrence. "Discourse and the Other: *The Third Life of Grange Copeland.*" Ed. Harold Bloom. *Modern Critical Views: Alice Walker.* New York: Chelsea House Publishers, 1989. (pp. 97-114).

hooks, bell. "Reconstructing Black Masculinity." *Black Looks: Race and Representation.* Boston: South End Press, 1992. (pp. 87-114).

Levin, David. *The Gay Novel in America.* New York: Garland Publishing Inc., 1991.

Mason, Jr., Theodore O. "Alice Walker's *The Third Life of Grange Copeland*: The Dynamics of Enclosure." *Callaloo.* 12.2. (1989). (pp. 297-309.)

McKay, Claude. "If We Must Die." *Selected Poems of Claude McKay*. New York: Bookman Associates, 1953. (p. 36).

Morrison, Toni. "Chloe Wofford Talks About Toni Morrison." *The New York Times Magazine*. September 11, 1994. (pp. 73-75).

Olney, James. "'I Was Born": Slave Narratives, Their Status as Autobiography and as Literature." *Callaloo* 7:1. (1984) (pp. 46-82).

Porter, Horace A. *Stealing the Fire: The Art and Protest of James Baldwin*. Middletown, Connecticut: Wesleyan University Press, 1989.

Savran, David. *Communists, Cowboys and Queers*. Minneapolis: University of Minnesota Press, 1992.

Sedgewick, Eve Kosofsky. *Epistimology of the Closet*. Berkeley: University of California Press, 1990.

Shakespeare, William. *The Tempest*. *The Riverside Shakespeare*. 1623 rpt Boston: Houghton Mifflin Company, 1974. (pp. 1606-1638).

"The Letter of Paul to the Romans." *The New Oxford Annotated Bible With the Apocrypha*. Eds. Herbert G. May and Bruce M. Metzger. New York: Oxford University Press, 1977. (pp. 1361-1379).

Walker, Alice. *Revolutionary Petunias and Other Poems*. New York: Harcourt Brace Jovanovich, 1973. (p. 65).

———. *The Third Life of Grange Copeland*. 1970 rpt. New York: Pocket Books, 1988.

Weatherby, W.J. *James Baldwin: Artist on Fire*. 1989 rpt. New York: Dell Publishing, 1990.

Wideman, John Edgar. *Brothers and Keepers*. 1984 rpt. New York: Penguin Books, 1985.

———. *Fatheralong*. New York: Pantheon Books, 1994.

———. *Philadelphia Fire*. New York: Henry Holt and Company, 12.2. (1990) (pp. 42-46).

———. "The Architectonics of Fiction." *Callaloo*. 1990. 13:1

Wright, Richard. "How 'Bigger' Was Born." Introduction to *Native Son*. 1940 rpt. New York: Harper and Row, 1989.

———. *Native Son*. 1940 rpt. New York: Harper and Row, 1989.

Yarborough, Richard. "Race Violence and Manhood: The Masculine Ideal in Frederick Douglass' 'The Heroic Slave.'" Ed. Eric Sundquist. *Frederick Douglass: New Literary and Historical Essays*. New York: Cambridge University Press, 1990. (pp. 166-188).

Index